MARCI ALBORGHETTI

THE PEOPLE
OF THE WAY OF
THE CROSS

Walking with Jesus through
the eyes of 14 witnesses

TWENTY
THIRD
PUBLICATIONS
www.23rdpublications.com

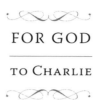

FOR GOD

TO CHARLIE

Scripture quotations are from New Revised Standard Version Bible, copyright ©1989 National Council of the Churches of Christ in the United States of America. Used by permission. All rights reserved.

TWENTY-THIRD PUBLICATIONS
1 Montauk Avenue, Suite 200, New London, CT 06320
(860) 437-3012 » (800) 321-0411 » www.23rdpublications.com

ISBN: 978-1-62785-063-6
Library of Congress Catalog Card Number: 2015955477
Printed in the U.S.A.

CONTENTS

INTRODUCTION

A few years ago, a good friend made a pilgrimage of sorts to the Holy Land. Being a newly minted Catholic as well as spiritually wise and technically proficient, she kept an astonishingly complete record of her experience there. The fact that she and her husband traveled under the auspices of Stanford University and had access to sites and people that the average tourist would not have experienced didn't hurt her record keeping.

She returned home with photos, movies, and realms of written material, and one evening at church, she presented a summary, an amazing travelogue that left her audience amazed at both her skills and her experience in Israel. What stood out most for me—and what I can't seem to forget even when I try—was the narrow, claustrophobic Way of the Cross.

My friend had had the opportunity not only to walk the Via Dolorosa, but to film it. Seeing the narrow path (it could not really be called a street) walled in on both sides, and hearing her narrate how Jesus would have stumbled along this way—sick and exhausted, carrying the weight of the cross, with nothing to protect him from the sometimes jeering crowd who had gathered along the way, a mere arm's length from him—literally made my skin prickle. It is one thing to imagine the Way of the Cross while safe in a darkened church surrounded by people you know and perhaps love, but it is quite another to witness the actual scene and to almost feel the walls closing in.

I began to think about what it would have been like, not only for Jesus, but for those in the crowd. Not all were his enemies. Some were merely curious, and others loved him and would have been horrified to see this painful spectacle, knowing full well how it would end. How did they feel when Jesus fell, not once or twice, but three times? How did they react when others mocked him and screamed and maybe even slapped and spit at him? What could they do with the constraints of the Roman soldiers and the vigilant eyes of the Jewish leaders upon them?

What would I have done?

What would you have done?

The next pages will show us how fourteen people, people just like you and me, might have reacted as they encountered Jesus on that first Good Friday. For every formal Station of the Cross, we will meet someone who might have been there. Some will be anonymous watchers; some will be historical figures that Scripture tells us were indeed present along the Way. All of them will be human beings like us: curious, frightened, devastated, uncertain, wondering. All but one who experienced Jesus along the Way could not have been sure, absent their faith, they were meeting their Savior. After all, one apostle had just betrayed him; another had denied him thrice. And yet each of them will be profoundly changed and moved by this short time with Jesus. Even in these hours before he died, spent and in excruciating pain, Jesus had the power to transform lives.

We, however, have an advantage over each of them with the possible exception of Mary: We *know* how this will all end, and it will not be in a shameful death by crucifixion, but in a glorious, life-giving resurrection. Because of this, we too are called to meet our Lord on the Way of the Cross and to each bear our own cross along with him.

Each of the following fourteen chapters will describe one of these encounters, corresponding to the particular Station of the Cross. Every chapter will offer a short discussion of how we can join the witness and experience the transformative power of Jesus on the road to Calvary. The chapters will close with a suggested prayer or action intended to bring us closer, on our own journey, to Jesus.

ONE

JESUS IS CONDEMNED TO DEATH

Pontius Pilate, The First Witness

Pilate asked him, "What is truth?" JOHN 18:38

I must make this quick. It's not that I don't want to spend another moment looking into this strange man's eyes. No, it's not that at all. There is nothing about him that frightens me. Of course not! How could there be? Just look at him! Defeated, pathetic, beaten. I've seen men come out of battle looking better than this one. He doesn't worry me. I just…I want…Ahh, why doesn't he look away? Why does he stare silently at me with that small, pained, sympathetic smile as if *he* is the one feeling sorry for *me*?

What is wrong with me? Why am I so distressed by this wretched man? His steady, sorrowful gaze makes it seem that the past few hours are crowding together in one long nightmare, just like the one that had troubled my wife earlier. This all started with her dream, a dream so violent that she sent word to me here at the praetorium even while I was sitting, ready to judge him. "Have nothing to do with that innocent man," she said, "for today I have suffered a great deal because of a dream about him" (Matthew 27:19).

When I heard her message, I felt a dread overtake me unlike anything I'd known before. It was ridiculous! I am not a man given to women's superstitions! I did not fight my way up in Caesar's esteem by showing myself to be weak! How could it be that I, who have ordered the deaths of so many, who have power of life and death over so many more, could be so plagued by this Jesus?

Through all this, the Jewish leaders have been demanding, insistent. They want him dead. And for what? Some ludicrous issues regarding their incomprehensible religion. It was insanity, and I'd wanted nothing to do with it. "You woke me for this?" I berated my centurion. Yet the chief priests were relentless. But what of Caesar? they asked, insinuating that this…this *Nazorene!* could be a problem for Caesar! That this Jesus, unwilling to even respond when I interrogated him, could challenge Caesar? I would have laughed had I not been so aggravated.

Had it not been for him.

As the chief priests prattle on, he stands unprotesting, watching. And whether it was my wife's dream or the strangeness of the man, I do not wish to condemn him. Why should I? I am not an animal, am I? Am I to be commanded by Jews? I see no reason for crucifixion in this case. Their complaints mean nothing to me, nothing to Rome, as long as I keep the taxes coming in and the Jews under control.

The priests have assembled quite a crowd, and now they begin to demand their traditional boon. Each year at their Passover festival, I, representing Caesar, representing Rome, am accustomed to freeing one prisoner for them. Certainly with all their vain rebellions and attempts to cheat Rome of its taxes, I have enough prisoners to offer them! But it suddenly occurs to me that this might be my chance to get rid of Jesus. Relief courses through me as I try to hide my eagerness.

"Do you want me to release for you the King of the Jews?" (Mark 15:9).

But no! Their leaders, consumed with jealousy at what this Nazorene has accomplished—just a few days ago I'd had reports of him drawing great crowds merely to watch him enter the city and hear him speak—stir up the crowd into a frenzy. They cry out for one of the Zealots, a rebel and murderer, named Barrabas. Unbelievable! These people! Less than a week ago they were lining up to praise this Jesus, and now they scream for his blood.

I turn away from the crowd, wheeling back to where Jesus stands, unsurprised at the mob's betrayal. I just observed the fear and hatred on the faces of the Jewish leaders when I called Jesus the King of the Jews. Unable to help myself, I stare at the Nazorene.

Silence, and then I can't keep silent. "So you are a king?"

The man finally speaks. "You say that I am a king. For this I was born, and for this I came into the world, to testify to the truth. Everyone who belongs to the truth listens to my voice."

I snort. "What is truth?"

I hide how much I want to know. But Jesus does not answer, and I am conscious of a stab of disappointment. But, really, how foolish of me! As if this one could define truth! What am I thinking, even to pose the question? How could this dirty, bloody Jew, with that appalling branch of thorns crushed onto his head, know anything about truth? If he knew the first thing about truth, he wouldn't be in this situation, would he?

Why, *why* do I want to snatch those thorns off his head?

I utter a groan and turn away from Jesus, but when I look away I am faced with the screaming crowd, goaded on by their chief priests, who are determined that this can only end one way. I wrench myself out of their sight, moving deeper into the shadows, pacing like a caged animal. Jesus does not move. He stands as patiently as an olive tree, bent and made ugly by its many years in the grove.

I can bear it no longer. These past few hours have seemed like days—years! My own people are watching me speculatively. They've never seen me so disturbed, so hesitant, so frustrated. Which of them is most eager to send a secret report to Caesar? I wonder bitterly. Enough! I've spent enough time on this Jew, these Jews with their ridiculous disputes. Time to get this over with.

But I want them to know, these bloodthirsty lunatics, that I am not part of their insanity. I am just doing what I must do as Caesar's governor. I have nothing against this one, this naïve preacher who got himself caught up in their games, caught between their leaders and Rome. I do not ascribe to their screams for vengeance. I simply must keep order, and that is why I will give them what they demand. They are not in control; they are not forcing *my* hand. I am governor!

Pilate strides into the open, lowers himself carefully onto the judgment seat, and looks out at the mob crying for this man's death. He feels chilled at the sight, knowing that he can do nothing short of killing them all to stop them from rioting, to stop word of this disaster from getting back to Rome. He sees his centurion grimace with disgust, but he is not sure whether it is at the crowd or his own hesitation. Pilate, seeing this man's disdain, feels as though a sword has entered his own back. He takes a deep breath and raises his hand for silence. Immediately, the crowd stops their clamor, but he can still see the rage twisting many faces.

But not all. Some appear confused, as if they'd come out on a bright, warm day for a festival and found themselves caught up in a violent thunderstorm. They gaze around at everything, dim and confused, unsure of what is happening. They look up at Jesus and then at him, wondering how things came to such a pass. But these are not the ones who attract Pilate's attention. He finds himself staring at the ones who have remained silent throughout this tumult. They have not raised a voice or a fist; they ignore the chief priests circulating through the crowd, and as if by unspoken agreement, those leaders keep back from these few while watching them closely. Their faces are contorted not by fury but by anguish. They do not look at him. They do not look at his soldiers. They do not even look at each other, although some of the women hold each other. They stare fixedly at Jesus, though he does not move or return their stares. Yet they cannot keep their eyes off of him, and there is a wretchedness in them that Pilate knows he will never forget. It is beyond pity, beyond sorrow, beyond fear, beyond even compassion.

It is beyond hope.

He has seen something like it only once before. On the way from Rome to Jerusalem, on that long, appalling journey to this miserable, ruinous place, he and his caravan passed a place where there had been several crucifixions. Nothing new there, just a demonstration of Roman might and justice. But his wife had called out for them to stop, and though she did not leave her draped conveyance, he saw her looking intently at the sight. He rode over to see what it was that had so captured her attention. Sitting at the foot of one of the trees used for the execution was a woman, no older than his wife. There was a boy hanging on the tree who had not yet reached full manhood, and he'd been dead for some time. Another foolish rebel, thought Pilate, and he was about to bid his wife to look away. But a slight wind stirred the woman's ragged veil and it fell away from her face.

Pilate saw that her eyes were steady upon the boy on the tree. There were no tears. She was as still as the rock she sat on. Five hundred soldiers and the new governor were not a stone's throw from her, dust flung into the air, the sound of horses and men, and yet she didn't even glance away from the boy. The only sign of life that Pilate could see was when she would close her eyes briefly against the burning sun, only to open them instantly as though worried that the child would need something and she might miss the word or gesture indicating what she could do for him. Her face, her eyes, bereft of hope and of life itself, told the world that she had died on that tree as surely as her child.

This is what Pilate now sees on these few faces focused on Jesus, and so he wrenches his eyes away, refusing to look upon them for even one more moment. He is not to blame for this! He motions for a bowl of water; after all, these Jews so love their cleansing rituals. They want purification? He will give them something to remember! He dips his hands into the water and then whips the drops over the crowd as he shouts, *"I am innocent of this man's blood!"* (Matthew 27:24).

But of course he knows he is not, nor ever will be. This is his wish, not his truth.

Pilate and Us

What do each of us have in common with Pontius Pilate?

Nothing! What a ridiculous question, right? How could any of us even consider having commonalities with Pilate, the villain who condemned Jesus to death? Surely the pressures he may have been under are no excuse for the horrifying role he played in Jesus' crucifixion. Had it been any one of us, we would have acted according to our better nature. We would have risen above any thought for our career, for the governorship we had purchased with hard-won, bloodstained money, for the esteem of our boss and colleagues and even subordinates, for any hope of a future of advancement, a future unstained by spectacular worldly failure. We would have gladly, easily, sacrificed all we had spent our life working to attain.

And if our boss was someone who could put us to death instead of just firing us, we still would have done right by Jesus. Right?

What is truth?

Pilate truly didn't know the answer. He may have posed the question in a seemingly cynical, apparently sarcastic manner, but as an educated, upper-class Roman, it was a real question for him. He would have known that the Greeks, from whom the Romans had co-opted much of their culture, had by that time been debating the question for centuries. And it's a good bet that Pilate had never asked this question of any prisoner before Jesus. Doing so would not have even occurred to him.

But Jesus was different. He was different for Pilate and he is different for us. He knows the truth. He is the Truth.

The gospels tell us that Jesus sent Pilate into a tailspin. None of the gospels suggest that Pilate merely played a functionary role in the crucifixion. He does not appear momentarily only to condemn. He has an actual exchange with Jesus, an ongoing dialogue. He is clearly torn about what to do. Pilate, whom history tells us was a successful soldier, a brutal politician, a strategist in every way, was shaken to the core by Jesus. The easiest thing for Pilate to have done would have been to condemn Jesus at dawn when the chief priests first approached him. This would have prevented a near riot in a notoriously volatile city, satisfied his political allies among the Jews, placated Herod, whose father had slaughtered upwards of two hundred boys in an effort to keep this king from surviving, and ensured that Caesar would have heard nothing of the incident.

But Pilate didn't do this. He wrangled with the situation, wrangled with the mobs, wrangled with Jesus, wrangled with his own soul and conscience. In the end, he did the expedient thing. Some believe he could have done no differently, given God's plan. But in choosing expediency over Jesus, is Pilate so very different from us? How far are we really willing to travel with Jesus down his path of radical love of God and others? How often do we play that part of pragmatist while unwittingly condemning his teachings—if not him—to a thousand little deaths?

What is truth?

Pilate didn't know the answer. Jesus did. Do we?

Action

Spend some time in contemplation. Consider all the ways in the past week in which you have acted the pragmatist instead of the radical Christian, all the times when you have followed the Pilates of the world instead of Jesus, when you have abandoned the search for truth and chosen what the world calls "realistic" thinking. Perhaps you have listened to or joined in a gossip session, hurried by someone begging for your spare change, chuckled uncomfortably at a racist or sexist story or joke, ignored or bullied a needy coworker or spouse, taken credit for another's work or bragged at the expense of someone else, blared your horn or gestured nastily at an inept or confused driver. The list goes on and on, from the mundane to the truly damaging decisions we make daily. List all the times you "pulled a Pilate." Select one or two and work on not repeating these actions in the coming week. Ask Jesus for help and courage in your effort.

Questions for Thought and Discussion

FOR PERSONAL REFLECTION

■ *What do you feel you need to control in your life? What do you suppose Jesus would say to you about this?*

■ *Has Jesus' immense love ever unsettled you, or made you uncomfortable? What did you do about it?*

FOR GROUP DISCUSSION

■ *Have you ever made an offer of care or concern that was misinterpreted by another? How can your community respond more fully to Jesus' love and concern for you?*

TWO

JESUS IS MADE TO BEAR THE CROSS

Dismas, A Thief to Be Crucified with Jesus, The Second Witness

Then two bandits were crucified with him,
one on his right and one on his left. MATTHEW 27:38

T he bandit with Dismas takes one look at Jesus and snorts. "He'll never even make it to Golgotha. That one can barely walk, never mind carry the cross."

Dismas eyes Jesus from below hooded lids that are bruised and swollen from the beating he has received from the Roman soldiers. His whole face throbs, but even though he and the other thief have been abused by their jailers, it is nothing next to what this one has endured. Dismas and the other watch from where they slump, their backs against the stone wall, waiting to be led along the path to where they will be crucified. This Jesus will be going with them, according to the soldiers who guard them. They are to wait for him.

Dismas is not accustomed to caring about other people, nor even thinking much about them, if he is being truthful with himself. He will sometimes make a halfhearted attempt to rationalize his stealing by saying that he does it to feed his wife and child, but he knows that is only a half-truth.

It *is* true, he tells himself defensively, that I could not make enough by working to pay the Roman taxes *and* feed my family. As it is, we barely have enough to eat, and we live in one crowded room. What do they expect a man to do when they bleed him of just about everything he earns?

But in his clearer moments, Dismas knows that something else drives his thievery. Anger. And not just at the Romans. As he watches Pilate wrangle with the crowd over this Jesus, Dismas feels the pain come flowing back into him from that day two years ago. He can almost see the midwife come out of the birthing place where his wife had been taken. The wizened old woman already had wrapped the tiny body. There was a blank look on her face as she confronted him.

"You had a son. Born dead. He almost took your woman with him. I told her last time, she should have no more, not try for a son. But you wanted a son."

He remembers hearing the condemnation in her voice, how she stared boldly into his eyes as she spoke, not changing her expression, not giving him any way to protest her words. His own eyes had fallen from hers to the bundle in her hands. His son. Born dead. And no chance for another. All he had dreamed of was to have a son who could work with him someday, perhaps on their own small bit of land, rather than as tenant farmers picking another man's grapes, another man's olives. But now there would be no chance of that. Dismas had walked away from the midwife, not caring about the disdain that was in her voice.

From that day on, he had found it more and more difficult to work the vineyards. His wife took so long to recover from the birth struggle that he had to leave his daughter with another man's wife while he went to the fields. God forgive him, he had come to resent the little girl—and to dislike the sight of his own wife as she lay, struggling to heal. There had been no healing in his little family after that day; they had not been together enough, and when his wife was well again, they'd barely talked.

"My fault," thought Dismas, his head aching from the Roman guards' blows. "And my fault what came next."

Dismas looked dully at his companion, the man who'd been caught stealing with him. They had met picking olives in the groves of a wealthy landlord. Dismas had not liked this man he would now die with—and he still did not like him. But Dismas couldn't help but listen to him. Always this one complained, always he talked about how wrong it was that so few had such wealth, and that the rest of them had to work like slaves to earn just a little; and then even that little, he always reminded Dismas, would be taken in taxes by the Roman pigs, that fat tyrant Pilate, the temple tax. His complaining was incessant, and frequently he would ask no one in particular: "Is this how Yahweh meant it to be? That his people should be slaves?"

The man's voice was like a drumbeat in Dismas' head;

after a while, he couldn't stop himself from listening, from asking the same questions but with some increasingly dark variations. "Is this what the Almighty meant for my life? To lose my only son before I could even know him?" Dismas would first ask in his mind and eventually, when no one was nearby, aloud. Soon, Dismas was no longer asking himself if Yahweh had forgotten him; he was telling himself that it was so.

This was the moment that the man who now crouched beside him, waiting to be crucified with him, was watching for, and when he saw that Dismas had lost hope in God and had given up on his better self, the man made his move. He took Dismas aside when meal times came for the workers and began to talk of how they could take back some of what Yahweh surely meant them to have in the first place. Gesturing to the landlord's fine home, he would tell Dismas, "Do you think he'll miss a little here or there? He has more than he knows what to do with, more than he'll ever need. Should he be the only one to benefit from the sweat of our bodies? Surely the Almighty wants us to have at least some part of the fruit of our labor?"

"I don't know what the Almighty wants," Dismas had finally answered grimly, "but I know what I need."

They had been successful at first, stealing fruit from whatever vineyard they were working, just enough to make them some extra money at the market, but not enough to arouse suspicion among the landlords or their overseers. But the man encouraged Dismas to grow bolder, and Dismas, believing that he had lost Yahweh's favor and knowing that he had lost the best part of himself on the day of his son's birth and death, grew reckless. The pair began to steal from a Bethany tax collector, a Jew who collected taxes for the Romans. Dismas had needed no further urging when his partner sneered, "Any Hebrew who robs his own people for the occupiers is worse than they are. Why should we not take back our own people's money?"

And keep it for ourselves? How are we any different from them? Dismas had thought but did not say. The truth was that by that time, he was beyond caring. The third time they robbed the tax collector, his employers were waiting. They were captured by Roman soldiers, pronounced guilty, and condemned to death. Pilate hadn't even bothered to see or hear them. The penalty for stealing from Rome was death, and they would be crucified to provide a gruesome lesson for any other potential Jewish thieves. Though he dreaded the excruciating pain of the next few hours, Dismas had reached the point where he couldn't wait for it to be done. He'd refused to see his wife when she'd come to the pit where they were held; he had the guards turn her away like a stranger. It was better for her that way, he told himself, better for the child. Perhaps her family would take them back if he made it clear that he'd rejected them. That she and his daughter would live out their lives in shame for what he'd done was not something he allowed himself to think about.

He huddled against the wall now, numb, weary, just wanting it all to be over.

And now this Jesus was prolonging the agony. Why is this taking so long? Why does the crowd care so much about what happens to this helpless rabbi? Why does the butcher Pilate waver so? Dismas turns his face again toward the beaten man standing a few cubits away. As he does, Jesus raises his eyes from where they are fixed upon the ground and looks at Dismas. Their eyes hold for just a moment, but Dismas feels as though he has been plunged into a deep, dark well of freezing water and then, just as abruptly, yanked back to the blindingly bright surface.

He gasps sharply as he feels life flow into him in a way that is almost unfamiliar. The day is instantly, piercingly bright, and Dismas feels that he is seeing everything anew, that just when he was most longing to die, he suddenly wants to live. And despite that impossible yearning in the face of death, he feels no grief. Despite his filthy clothes and unwashed body, he feels clean.

Who is this Jesus?

Though himself a target for the contempt of others, Dismas cannot understand the rage he has seen in the past hour directed toward this man. Dismas tries to recall what he knows about Jesus. It has been so long since Dismas has cared about anything, but even he has heard the rumors about a Nazorene enraging the Sanhedrin while simultaneously winning the loyalty of the people. Dismas had seen the adoring crowds attending Jesus when he entered the temple just a few days ago through the East Gate. Had there been cries of Messiah and Christ? Dismas is now ashamed to remember that he was more interested in planning the next theft from the tax collector than in seeing the man who inspired such rejoicing.

Yet here he is, and no one is rejoicing now. How have these people been made to turn on the one they adored a mere few days before? Dismas gazes curiously out over the crowd and, with newly sharpened senses, realizes that not all are against Jesus. There are faces among the enraged mob that are lined with agony for this wretched man. But violent men have taken control of the crowd, and Dismas can see members of the Roman guard with clerks of the Sanhedrin urging on those who are screaming the loudest.

In an instant, it is over. Pilate gives them what they scream for, and the centurion orders Jesus to take up the cross. Dismas feels a sickness rising in him.

"Watch this," sneers the thief next to Dismas. "He'll never even lift it. We'll probably get stuck carrying it for him."

But as Dismas watches, his heart hammering in his chest, Jesus does lift it. He grasps the wood and, slowly, painfully, raises it to rest on his shoulder. As Jesus begins to walk with the cross upon him, he gazes once more at Dismas. Again Dismas feels something extraordinary, but this time it is an exquisite, searing pain as though a knife is tearing through his body and soul. When, after an instant that feels like a lifetime, the pain fades, Dismas understands that the bitterness in him has been cut away. He hears a faint echo of the question he's been asking for years: "Where is God for me?"

And Dismas, dragging his own cross behind Jesus, knows exactly where God is for him.

Dismas and Us

We all want to be like Dismas, the bandit crucified beside Jesus who turned to our Lord on the cross and who was later named a saint for that crucifixion conversion. It's not that we all want to be thieves, but more that we all know at some level that we are sinners. At some level, we fail Jesus; and if we know that we fail Jesus, we also want to be comforted by the knowledge that we will be forgiven by

Jesus. So Dismas is a dream come true for us! Not only has
he been a really bad guy (much worse than any of us!), he's
committed a crime that warrants the death penalty. And if
this guy, this rogue, this bandit, this terrible troublemaker,
can win God's forgiveness with a few words, well then, certainly we'll be OK!

But do we really believe this? Do we really believe, deep
down in our hearts and way up in our heads, that God
forgives even deathbed—or in the case of Dismas, crucifixion—penitents? Do we believe that deathbed penitents
deserve forgiveness? After all, they let it go right down to
the wire, didn't they, presumably sinning for all they were
worth until it was almost too late? Do we really believe that
Jesus will forgive us when push comes to shove?

God's radical forgiveness is often difficult for us to accept, probably because we know we could never manage to
forgive so utterly. I was only eleven or twelve when a young
priest came to our parish to assist our older and, it must
be said, curmudgeonly pastor. Vatican II was in play, and
this young man must have taken courage from that, or he
was simply brave and zealous. One of his first sermons was
on forgiveness. I remember my head snapping up when he
proclaimed that, for all we knew, God had forgiven Hitler.
Mine wasn't the only case of whiplash that Saturday evening, and a lot of nerves and muscles and tendons much
older than mine had apparently been strained by that
young priest's words. Somehow he managed to ride out the
storm, because it was several years before he left us, but
I've never forgotten that sermon.

Did God forgive Hitler? If Hitler, like Dismas, was truly
repentant and understood that he was experiencing God's

presence, then there can be no doubt that God forgave Hitler.

The more important question for each of us is this: Can I *accept and embrace* God's forgiveness right now and forevermore?

Prayer

Jesus, Lord, I ask you not only for forgiveness, which I need anew every moment of every day, but also for the grace to accept your pure and blessed forgiveness. Teach me to have the humility, Lord, to realize that none of my sins are bigger than your mercy. Nothing I could do is so important that it would change your merciful nature. Jesus, help me to understand that embracing your forgiveness is not the same as denying my sin, but that my sin is obliterated in the bright light of your mercy. Thank you, Lord! Amen.

Questions for Thought and Discussion

FOR PERSONAL REFLECTION

▨ *Who needs forgiveness in your life? A family member? Spouse? Coworker? You? Imagine this person, alone, facing Jesus. What do you see in Jesus' eyes as he speaks to them? What do you wish to say to this person, in Jesus' presence?*

FOR GROUP DISCUSSION

Is it ever possible to justify a refusal to forgive?

How can your community practice forgiveness and respect for all?

THREE

JESUS FALLS THE FIRST TIME

A Small Child, The Third Witness

Then little children were being brought to him in order that he might lay his hands on them and pray. MATTHEW 19:13

Startled, the child opens her eyes wide and stares. The strange man has fallen down right beside her! At the same time that she opens her eyes, she closes her mouth, for she has been wailing in terror for her mother, from whom she has somehow become separated. They were walking together when the crowd came rushing down the narrow road, and though her mother had grasped for her hand, it was too late. The little one had not been paying attention, and, curious about where all the people had come from and what they were doing, she'd let herself be swept away from her mother.

It had never occurred to her that her mother could vanish so quickly.

Her shrieks had been ignored by the people suddenly surrounding her, and since her high-pitched voice was loud enough in her own ears, this surprised her. And now this man! Right in front of her! She is a bold child, this little one, and brave, though her poor mother has had moments when she wished otherwise.

Instantly, her terror is replaced by wonder, no longer just at the roiling mob of people but at this man. She wonders if he could be her father. She has heard many times when she should not have been listening, when those talking presumed she could not understand, that her father was a bad man who left her mother and her alone to fend for themselves. But her mother tells her always that her father went away to work in another country, and she believes her mother. Most of the time. She is not quite sure. If he really loved them the way his mother says, why is he not with them? She has heard her grandmother, who is angry all the time, whisper to her mother that her father has ruined them, that her mother will never find a good husband now. She wants her father to come back and prove that her grandmother is wrong. She does not remember what he looks like. She does not know if she has ever even seen him. She is only five years old.

Is this man her father?

She looks closely at Jesus, fallen into a painful crouch on his knees right beside her. His face is on the same level as hers. As she stares at his dirty face and tangled hair, she hears a soft groan. This man is hurt! She is surprised to see that his face is bruised and cut. Slowly, as if it hurts him to do it, he looks into her eyes. And he gives her a very small, sad smile.

He is not her father! She remembers now, studying his poor face so closely. This was the man who had held her up in the air and laughed with her and the other children a few days ago! He is so different now that she hadn't recognized him until she saw his eyes and smile. Her mother had brought her to the market in Jerusalem to buy some of the things they needed for Passover. While they were hurrying along, a friend of her grandmother had seen them and come rushing up to them. "Come with me! He is here, and they say he is blessing the children," the older woman had told them breathlessly. "Would it not be good to have him bless your little one?"

Her mother had seemed uncertain, but the older woman had pushed and pulled them along until they turned a corner, and the little girl had seen him—this same man!—in the middle of a group of laughing, shouting children, many her age and some even smaller. Her grandmother's friend had pushed her forward into the group, and though her mother had opened her mouth as if to call her back, she didn't. So the little girl had stepped bravely into the group of children, and before she knew it, the man had turned to her. He swept her up into his arms as she had seen him do with other children and swung her about, laughing and naming her a child of God, a child of Abba, Father in heaven. She was delighted and not in the least bit afraid. He was very happy, but the men around him were not happy. One of them looked at her the way her grandfather did when she chattered away at him while he was busy.

The men with him had scolded her and the other children, telling their mothers to take them away, but Jesus said, "Let the little children come to me, and do not stop them; for it is to such as these that the kingdom of heaven belongs" (Matthew 19:14). Then he had given the children one last smile, so much more joyful than the one he gave her now, and went away with the stern men.

As the little girl remembers all this, someone behind Jesus, a soldier, kicks him in the side, and the girl sees a spasm of pain pass over Jesus' face. But even then, he tries to keep the small smile as if he does not want her to be frightened. She is not frightened. She is angry at the soldier, angry at all these people for hurting and shouting at the man who had so delighted her. She feels sorry for him. She wishes that he *was* her father and that she could push the wood off his shoulder and lead him away from this place. She wishes that he would drop the wood and swing her up onto his shoulder, and that they would run away from this crowd *right now!*

But she can see that this will not happen. She can see that he has changed since she saw him a few days ago. Then he was so strong and seemed so merry. Now he is weak, pale, and sad, despite the smile. Then he was free, now he is bound to these soldiers; and even as he reaches out a trembling finger to touch her face, he is being dragged to his feet, although for a moment he cannot seem to find them underneath him. The heavy wood is pushed back upon him, and he starts to drag it forward.

Slowly, slowly, she watches him move away from her, and the angry people go with him. She watches, wanting to call him back, knowing that he cannot come back to her. Before she remembers that she is lost and starts to wail again, she feels quick, strong arms snatch her up, and she is holding onto her mother's neck and they are following Jesus.

The Small Child and/In Us

It is very popular, psychologically speaking, to refer to the little boy or the little girl in each of us as our "inner child." The idea, much simplified, is that what happens to us—or doesn't happen to us—when we are young is certain to mark each of us to some degree or another. If we have emotional or spiritual or even physical problems later on, in adulthood, these may be traced back to these early years. If such early experiences can be appropriately identified and accurately connected to our problems as adults, they can often be addressed. People who might have been deeply hurt in early childhood may be encouraged to "get in touch with the child inside" and to let that child know that she or he is lovable, good, and worthwhile.

Perhaps one of the reasons we are so vulnerable—to both hurt and goodness—in our early years is that we are so innocent; certainly we are inexperienced in the ways of the world. Deceit, greed, cruelty, and idolatry are all basically unknown to us, particularly in their darkest permutations. This may well be why Jesus makes several references to the kingdom of heaven belonging to little children, and why he advises adults to become like little children so that they can accept and enter God's kingdom. A small, healthy child who has not yet been taught the "ways of the world" is open, curious, brave, and most of all, *interested* in everything. That is what Jesus, as God and with God, is looking for in and from those who would seek and find the kingdom of God.

As with the small children he blesses in the gospels, he is looking for us to be open to him and his teachings. He wants us to be bravely curious in the Word, in the Father, and in the Holy Spirit. He seeks those who are eager to be with him, for no other reason *than* to be with him, just as a child hankers to be with a friend or relative she or he loves.

Another way in which we must find the child in ourselves to grow closer to God and the kingdom is to remember how helpless small children are. From infants who can't do even the smallest thing for themselves, to toddlers and preschoolers who look to adults to meet all of their expressed and unexpressed needs—we are that young in relation to God, although we often forget it or refuse to admit it. And that, Jesus is saying when counseling us to be like children, is where we make our mistakes. I think it unlikely that God is impressed by our so-called, much-touted independence, especially when it borders on arrogance and pride.

We are to become like little children in acknowledging our complete dependence on the Almighty no matter how counterintuitive it is for us, as adults, to admit such helplessness. Small children know they need the adults in their lives, but as they get older, they rebel against this need. They want to do things on their own: dress themselves, walk outside without holding Dad's hand, get on the bus without kissing Mom good-bye, not eat their carrots. This, of course, is the process of growing up. But with God, our "growing up" is a delusion we convince ourselves of in order to feel more in control. Ask any believer who has experienced serious illness or tragedy, and she or he will tell you just how much control we have over our lives in the long run. To enter peacefully and peaceably into God's kingdom, we must acknowledge and embrace the fact that it's God's kingdom for a reason: God rules!

Finally, little children have a quality or a characteristic that is too often drained out of us as we age. They expect good things! Until they find out otherwise—until they are denied too often and too angrily—they expect that life's gifts are all for them. They expect that the people around them are always happy to be with them and to grant their every wish. They expect that the sun will shine, and the water will be warm, and that nothing will hurt them. They expect that when they ask for a piece of candy, they will get it—just watch the naked hope in their faces!

Those small children who went to Jesus to be blessed expected him to welcome them, as he did. Note that it was the adults—even the apostles and disciples, who should have known better—who grumbled and grouchily tried to stop the children from coming to Jesus. It's actually an amusing Scripture passage when actually visualized: secretly jealous of the love their master showers on little kids who so clearly expect to get that love, these disciples use the excuse of Jesus' greatness and importance to try to prevent the very sort of action that makes him great: expressing love for us.

And that's precisely where entering the kingdom of God differs from entering the world of responsible adulthood: the world of adulthood is filled with duties and obligations and, most of all, the resounding and too-often-repeated word "No!" So much in our adult lives, we've learned, is not good for us. But when we joyfully approach God's kingdom, we go in expecting wondrous, amazing, miraculous things. God's love for us is all about "Yes!" Because everything about God is good for us.

Action

Imagine the kingdom of God from the perspective of a child—if possible, through the eyes of the "child in you," or at least through the memory of the child you were before the world began to dim and constrain your expectations. Think about every physical need you have, and then imagine it being met or, if it is a negative need like an addiction, imagine it gone and never troubling you again. Consider every question you've ever had about anything, and imagine it being answered. Feel the weight of every sin or offense or doubt, and imagine it lifted. Remember all the long shadows in your life—whether from short winter days or a hurting heart—and imagine them shimmering with light. Admit the power of fear and anxiety in your life, and imagine it utterly dissipated. Confront the loss of every loved one and wonderful spirit in your life, and imagine each of them with you. Recognize the source of every bit of sorrow and emptiness you've ever felt, and imagine this source—your yearning for God—completely met. Forever. Try to retain these "imaginings" as you live your life; make an effort to spend at least a few minutes each day as a child in the kingdom of God.

Questions for Thought and Discussion

FOR PERSONAL REFLECTION

What frightens you right now? Can you picture yourself bringing this fear to Jesus? What does he say to you about it?

FOR GROUP DISCUSSION

In what ways has your image of God changed over the years from your childhood to adulthood?

FOUR

A Mother Caught Up in the Crowd, The Fourth Witness

Then Simeon blessed them and said to his mother Mary,
"This child is destined for the falling and the rising of many
in Israel, and to be a sign that will be opposed so that the inner
thoughts of many will be revealed—and a sword will pierce
your own soul too." **Luke 2:34–35**

She hardly knows what she is doing.

She'd been so afraid when her little girl's hand had floated out of her reach! Then when the crowd pushed its way between them, she could hear her child shrieking, and she knew she would do anything to get to her. She clawed and pushed back and even dropped the jar of olive oil her mother had sent her to buy for the special meal tonight. She heard the jar breaking as it hit the ground without even worrying about her mother's anger at the lost oil or wasted money.

She screamed her child's name, but the crowd that had appeared in this narrow way was uncontrollable, feral. What were they doing? Not a moment before, this narrow street had been quiet, almost strangely so, as if everyone was hidden, waiting for something to happen. It had been so calm that she'd let her headstrong daughter have her way and run just a bit ahead of her. That child was so determined to show her will and yet so sweetly open-natured that it was a constant challenge to keep her safe and under control. And her own mother wasn't helping, constantly whispering in her angry, hissing voice that the child was just like her father and would go the same way if not strictly contained.

"It will be hard enough to marry her off some day, what with her father abandoning you," her mother had chided just this morning before sending her off on yet another errand. "And yet you indulge her as though she has every advantage!"

As much as she resented her mother's nagging, and as much as she secretly loved her child's strong will, her mother had been proven right yet again. For hadn't she just lost her little daughter in the crowd because she'd given in to the little one's determination to walk on her own?

But who could have expected this crowd? Where had they come from so suddenly? Why were they here? On Passover no less! Her heart froze when she thought that it might be another rebellion, the Zealots trying to provoke the Sanhedrin or Rome during the festival. No! She could not lose her little girl in the midst of one of their violent protests. Not long ago, the Romans, trying to put down just such a rebellion, had killed hundreds of Jews. And on Passover it would be even worse! Her father had said that the Roman prefect, a man named Pilate, would do anything to keep peace in Jerusalem, especially during the festival. He was said to be a brutal man who made no effort to fairly rule, or even understand, the Jews.

And there were so many people in Jerusalem and the surrounding region during Passover. On her way to and from the city over the past week, she had witnessed the tents and makeshift shelters appearing overnight to house those pilgrims who had come for the festival but had not been able to find lodging. Thousands of them! And some of them dangerous, she thought, terrified for her child. The young mother knew that not all of them would be like the man she'd met earlier in the week, the kind, good-hearted rabbi so many had come to see. In fact, having seen him, she doubted there was anyone in Jerusalem quite like him.

Her first thought when she'd seen Jesus among all those children was, *Is **he** the one causing such a stir*? He did not look like any rabbi she'd ever seen, and certainly not any Pharisee or Sadducee! He was too young and raggedly dressed to be an elder. He was taking such delight in the children, and that was another thing she'd never witnessed in any of the Jewish leaders. She wasn't sure she'd ever seen any of them even near a child who was not their own. They had grown too important, too aware of their own importance, too deeply involved in appeasing Pilate and the Romans, to spend much time among their own agitated people.

Yet this Jesus was known for staying among the people; it was said that he ate and drank and stayed with even known sinners. Her parents had been disdainful of what they heard of him, but she had not been so sure. Perhaps if more of their own leaders attended to the needs of the people, there would not be such confusion, such despair. There had been nothing of despair about the man that day as he lifted the children into the air, blessing her own laughing little one with the rest.

But when she returned later that day—without telling her mother where she was going—to hear him teach, she'd seen another side to Jesus. He spoke well, intently, and held the crowd closely. Unlike the temple priests and rabbis, Jesus encouraged the crowd to speak, to ask questions. He answered each of them, even when his words did not please them. She remembered how surprised she'd been when a woman in the crowd raised her voice and said to him, "Blessed is the womb that bore you, and the breasts the nursed you!" But he said, "Blessed rather are those who hear the word of God and keep it!" (Luke 11:27–28).

There had been another woman that day, standing near Jesus, and as soon as he said those words, her face had fallen for just an instant, before she lifted it again with a wry, knowing smile. *It is his mother*, she'd thought instantly, recognizing, as only a mother can, the kind of swift, momentary pain one's child can inflict with just a word or a look. Jesus had done it publically; yet the older woman had reacted wonderfully. Whatever she may have felt, she showed no sign of embarrassment or even irritation. As Jesus continued to speak, she watched attentively, as any mother would, though like any mother listening to her child, she'd probably heard it all many times before.

Now frantic to reach her own child, whose cries she can no longer hear, the young mother suddenly realizes why the mob has materialized around them. The Romans are crucifying rebels! During the festival? How could even Pilate command this during Passover? As panicked as she is about her daughter, the thought chills her. What is to become of her people if they can be treated in such a way?

And then all thoughts empty from her mind because someone in front of her shifts and she sees her child.

Kneeling by a prisoner fallen under his cross.

Her breath stops. Her throat burns with a silent scream. She is several yards behind, and from what she can see, her brave, heedless child is trying to help the condemned man. A Roman soldier extends his leg to kick the prisoner. Or her child.

She does not wait to find out which. Strength unlike anything she'd imagined possible surges through her. She leaps forward, avoiding a blow from another guard. Now she is behind her child, snatching her back and away from the fallen man, from the cruel cohort marching him toward death.

She is shocked when her daughter looks at her with clear, shining eyes, not a bit afraid. Wrapping her arms around her mother's neck, the little one leans forward and whispers, "It's him! The laughing man who said I was God's child!"

For a long, confusing moment, her mother does not comprehend. Her own heart is beating so fast, the blood rushing in her ears, the noise of the crowd all around her. Then, searching her daughter's excited face, she understands. She glances up swiftly, just in time to see them drag him to his feet, and as she watches, he turns and looks into her eyes for one instant. Then they shove the young rabbi forward.

Without even willing it, she slowly follows, her daughter clinging to her neck. Though the crowd sweeps them along, she feels she cannot turn back now even if she wants to. It is as if she is in a dream that she may not wake from without seeing it through to the end. She does not even think about what her mother will say.

Abruptly the crowd goes silent. The sudden quiet is as jarring as the shouting and pushing had been, and she stretches to see what has happened. Up ahead, Jesus has stopped, and even the cohort seems to hesitate around him. A woman steps forward, coming very near to him, a woman bent with sorrow, her face barely visible. But the young mother sees enough to know that this is his mother, the woman she'd seen in the crowd who had taken his words to heart and then let them go.

Like the rest of the crowd, the young mother is mesmerized. She cannot stop watching. She sees the woman speak a few words, bow her head, and sob. Jesus leans forward until his forehead, scratched and bleeding from the thorns, is just touching the top of hers. His eyes close. He does not speak.

As if unable to bear the sight of such anguished tenderness, the guard who had kicked Mary's son now wrenches him away from her. Mary swiftly reaches out her arms as if to draw him back, but Jesus smiles, shakes his head once, and turns away from her.

The young mother feels her child's small, soft hand upon her cheek.

"Mama, why are you crying?"

The Young Mother and Us

It can seem hard for us to understand Jesus. His life and
teachings, while showing us the path to life, can also feel
a bit confusing, even contradictory, at times. We are like
the young mother in this: The more we try to know Jesus,
the more we realize that he was much more complicated
than we might wish. After all, Jesus was God on earth, the
Creator among the creatures, joined with humanity; if that
seems complicated for us, we cannot even imagine how it
was for him!

How many of us have wondered, with the young mother, how Jesus could have seemingly dismissed Mary in
answering the woman who cried out a blessing for his
mother from the crowd? At various times the gospels reveal Jesus as both the defiant son and the obedient son.
We see Jesus frightening his parents when at the young
age of twelve he stayed behind in Jerusalem after Mary and
Joseph had long since begun the journey back to Nazareth,
only to then follow them home and do their bidding for,
evidently, the next eighteen years. We see him all but telling Mary to mind her own business when she tells him
at the Cana wedding about the lack of wine, only to then
change the water into wine. We see him refusing to even
receive his family when they come to talk to him, and yet
we know that he often traveled with Mary.

Other gospel descriptions of Jesus' words and actions
can appear disconcerting. He chastises Peter, instructing
him to forgive a multiplicity of sins, yet he tears into those
who are trading money and selling sacrifices in the temple—Jews who are, really, just following their traditions.
He tells his disciples that he embodies the forgiveness of

sins, but then warns them that if they don't love one another and care for the poor, they will not enter the kingdom of heaven.

But for all of the complications and challenges presented by Jesus' teachings and by the gospel portrayals of Jesus as a man, there is nothing confusing about Jesus on the road to Golgotha. This is what he has come to do. This is how he saves us. This is the road we must take with him—compelled, as the young mother is compelled, but not by the crowd or the drama of the moment. We are compelled by knowing what she cannot know: that Jesus is on this road for us, that Jesus is about to die for us. To show us that God is real and among us. To prove the love that he says must abide in us.

And so we bear witness to this excruciatingly wrenching moment between human mother and divine/human son. Every moment of the three-plus decades before this instant have been leading to this. Only this woman can truly know what he is suffering, physically, emotionally, and spiritually. Jesus, man, is looking into the eyes of the one person on earth who is conceivably suffering more than he is. He knows it. She knows it. While he is doing this *for* us, he is doing it for, but also to, her. This moment is an acknowledgment. And then, for our sakes, he walks on.

Prayer

*Mary, mother of Jesus, in this moment you suffer uniquely
and yet as every woman suffers to see her child suffer. You
make this agonizing sacrifice for the sake of the world, but
how much could that mean to you as you looked into the
frightened, sorrowful, pain-filled eyes of your son? Help
me, Mary, as I try to stand beside you in this moment,
to understand that whatever small sacrifices I make for
my child, my mother, my father, my sister, my brother, my
neighbor, are nothing compared to your sacrifice, and yet
they are the least that your sacrifice demands. Give me just
a fraction of the courage that passed between you and your
son that dark morning, and let my courage lead to a bright
new day as yours did. Amen.*

Questions for Thought and Discussion

FOR PERSONAL REFLECTION

*Which of Jesus' teachings is particularly hard for you to
follow? What can you do to understand this teaching
more deeply and make it your own?*

FOR GROUP DISCUSSION

*Looking at Jesus' relationship to his mother, how are
some of the relationships in your community or family
similar or different? How might they be improved?*

FIVE

JESUS IS HELPED BY THE CYRENEAN

Simon, The Fifth Witness

They compelled a passer-by, who was coming in from the country, to carry his cross; it was Simon of Cyrene, the father of Alexander and Rufus. **MARK 15:21**

Simon sees the mob seething in the narrow street ahead and sighs. How will I push through this mass of people? he wonders as he approaches the place where his path will cross theirs. What are they doing out in such numbers with just a few hours until the Passover Sabbath? Have they no preparations to make? No respect for Yahweh's commands?

Then he catches a glimpse of Roman armor, and his sigh becomes a spark of rage. Another execution! During our holiest days! These pagan Romans are animals. Of all the times in the year that they have to crucify—and do crucify—Jews and other foreigners, must they practice their

43

barbarism today? The Romans had already overrun his own city, Cyrene, giving the Greeks leave to oppress his fellow Jews as they have wished to do for centuries. Even so, a Jew from anywhere in the world should be able to find solace in Jerusalem, God's city. Yet what has he found here in Jerusalem?

The Roman foot is firmly on the throat of Judaism, oppressing the Jews who make their home here, and corrupting even some of the priests as they tread the thin line between appeasing the Romans and being seduced into their paganism. Oh, there are many good Jewish leaders who resist the Romans and their obscene empire; Simon knows this. But there are also those who are all too willing to eat and drink with the idol worshipers, to share in the bounty of Roman wealth, to support Caesar's edicts and taxes, and to erect the Roman eagle, a symbol of their pagan power, even in the temple precincts! Those are the Jews whom Simon and his sons, Alexander and Rufus, cannot help but despise. Those are the leaders who reap what they sow in availing themselves of the Roman bounty. Those are the ones who have truly betrayed their people, not these wretches who are crucified almost daily for whatever resistance they manage to make to Roman rule.

Simon is from a pious family, dedicated to Yahweh and his laws and anxiously awaiting his Messiah who will cleanse his people of these oppressors and the Jews who have been corrupted by them. He and his sons had joined the community of Jewish exiles in Cyrene, welcomed without regard for the color of their skin or the fact that they made their home among the farmers of North Africa. But Roman rule had changed the lives of Jews from Rome to

Antioch and now, as he has discovered, Jerusalem as well.
Even the holy city has been tainted.

However, Simon has learned the value of silence. He
knows the grave danger of open rebellion against the
Romans, and even against the Jewish leaders who have
made themselves into Roman lackeys. He feels the strain
of having sons who would fight, and his constant restraint
of Alexander and Rufus has caused tension in his once
peaceful home. Hot to fight the Romans in any way they
can, his sons have resisted and, finally, resented his efforts
to keep them safe. Angered at the corruption of their own
leaders, they yearn to express their faith through violence,
but Simon has fearful visions of his two sons crucified like
the Zealots and the other rebels. And so he counsels them
to wait, to be patient, to remember Yahweh's promise of a
Messiah to free his people Israel and speak God's truth to
the world.

But Alexander and Rufus—and, if he is honest with
himself, he too—have grown tired of waiting. Who is to say
when Yahweh's Messiah will come? Who is to say that he
is not already here, waiting for the right time to vanquish
the Romans? Perhaps he is even now laying plans, preparing his followers for the kingdom. This is the argument
his sons, particular Rufus, make against Simon's plea for
patience.

"Father, what if the Messiah is here now, waiting for us
to show our willingness to join him? What if he is waiting
for his people to prove themselves ready?"

Simon is too experienced in the ways of men to risk
the lives of his sons on such speculation, though he prays
daily for Yahweh's Messiah to come, to show some sign to

his people. To pacify his sons, however, he planned this pilgrimage to Jerusalem for the Passover festival. It had been more than a decade since they'd made the journey together, the last time when Rufus was still a boy. It would do the three of them some good, Simon had thought, and they could afford to spend the time away from their farm. Over the years he'd grown successful enough to hire good hands and good managers, and although Simon was still a strong man who worked in the fields along with his men and women, he knew he didn't need to be on the land every day.

He'd hoped that if they could spend this Passover in Jerusalem, away from the roiling anger of the young Jews in Cyrene, he could show his sons the greatness of the temple, the depth of the relationship between the Jews and Yahweh, the history of their people. To experience Passover in the holy city, he'd thought, would show his sons that the path of God's chosen people was not rooted in violence and hatred, but in faith. Perhaps such a pilgrimage would turn his sons' hearts away from the violent rebellion that could prove fatal for them. It was with great and almost desperate hope that he'd taken lodgings for the three of them, not far from the temple.

But Jerusalem had not proved the remedy Simon had sought. It had changed in the years since they'd last visited. The Roman stamp was more visible; their influence could be seen everywhere. Some of the Jewish leaders openly collaborated with Pilate and his people. The high priest was rumored to communicate regularly with Pilate about keeping the Jews in line. Everywhere Simon and his sons looked, they saw money-traders, tax collectors, the

Roman eagle, Herodian architecture. Where was the pure faith Simon had been seeking? Where was the devotion to Yahweh? Where were the hearts genuinely seeking the Messiah?

And now this! This blasphemy—crucifixion on the holy day of Passover! A man accustomed to using his body, he had gone into the country around Jerusalem at dawn to walk and observe and work away some of his frustration and disappointment. There was still a chill from the long night in the air as he returned to Jerusalem and encountered the mob accompanying the crucifixion procession. What were all these people doing here so early in the day? What made these victims any more interesting than the hundreds, the thousands, the Romans had already crucified?

As the procession approached, leading out of Jerusalem toward Golgotha, Simon peered closely at the crowd. His heart shuddered. Rufus was there, in the midst of the chaos. Instantly Simon's eyes scanned the other men in the crowd, but his firstborn, Alexander, was not among them. This brought little relief. What was Rufus thinking? After all the discussions they'd had, all the warnings he'd given, yes, even the threats, here was his youngest in this most dangerous place in all of Jerusalem. He tried to catch Rufus' eye, but his son's gaze was fixed on one who carried a cross between two others.

Hardly able to tear his eyes away from his son, Simon glanced at the man who had so captured Rufus' attention. There was nothing remarkable to see at first glance. He was bent and bloody, having been flogged, and blood still flowed from the wounds that had been opened by this brutal journey. Then, through a tangle of bloody, sweat-soaked hair into which thorns were woven, the man looked up. His gaze fixed upon Simon, and now Simon felt that he could not breathe. There was something here that he could not understand, but that thrilled every fiber of his being. Simon could not look away, even as he began to feel the man's agony in his own body. And while still lost in Jesus' gaze, Simon felt the hard, heavy, implacable hand of the centurion on his shoulder. Simon found himself looking into eyes as dead as Jesus' were alive.

"Lift the cross behind him," was all the centurion said before shoving Simon toward the man.

And now Rufus did indeed see his father.

Simon and Us

In my parents' ancient Bible, there is an evocative depiction of Simon being instructed to take up the cross behind Jesus. He has a very empathetic demeanor and a sorrowful look upon his face. He appears in most of the remaining illustrations of the Stations, leaving the distinct impression that he couldn't manage to leave the Lord even after they arrived at Golgotha. It is a comforting image. It allows us to think that there was at least one person in the nightmare of the crucifixion who actually wanted to—and did— help Jesus.

But Scripture makes it clear that Simon wasn't exactly a volunteer. He must be compelled to help Jesus, forced into the service. And who among us could blame him? What decent person wants to be involved in such a situation? What kind of individual would jump at the chance to be forever after identified with someone sentenced to death

by both religious and secular law? Add to those objections
the fact that Simon was likely a visitor in Jerusalem, probably there for Passover, and possibly a country man who
would not have been accustomed to the cacophony of ur-
ban life. He knew the power of Rome, both in his home of
Cyrene (in modern Libya) and even more so in Jerusalem.
He would have wanted nothing more than to keep his head
down and get out of the situation.

When you were in school and the teacher asked a question, how did you react? I invariably ducked my head and
cast my eyes down, hoping that I would be passed over. I
did this even when I was absolutely certain of the answer. I
didn't want the attention. It seemed enough of a burden to
me just getting through school, getting good grades, navi-
gating the social ins and outs. To volunteer to speak up, to
volunteer to make a spectacle of myself! was just unthink-
able to me.

I think that may be our first inclination when we are
asked to help Jesus carry his cross today. And, believe me,
we *are* asked, every minute of every day, to in some way
help with that burden. The easiest response is to duck our
heads and hope that God will pass us by, or more accurately, give us a pass. It is difficult to step out of the line,
to put ourselves forward, to make ourselves available. It
can be embarrassing. Surely it was for Simon. Suddenly,
he was not the frightened man creeping along the edges of
the crowd; he was the veritable center of attention. When
a beggar asks us for money or food or even conversation,
it is much easier to scurry away and hope that others don't
notice how we were singled out, particularly if the beggar
is loud or unattractive or dirty. When someone in line at

the grocery store or pharmacy is in evident distress, we tell ourselves that reaching out or even offering a direct sympathetic look is intrusive and not "minding our own business." When a neighbor is struggling to get his trash out to the curb, we are quick to think about how unsanitary the garbage is and how late we already are.

In one way, helping Jesus carry the cross was a much easier decision for Simon. He really didn't have a choice. He was forced into service. We are given a choice. We can respond to God's call to help with the cross, or we can fall back into the comfortable shadows of our lives.

Action

Be conscious of the opportunities God gives you to respond to his call to help carry Jesus' cross. Be aware of how often you are asked on a daily basis to help bear another's burden. Monitor your reaction when this happens. Is your first inclination to help carry that cross, or to draw away and hide yourself? Does your reaction vary depending upon the circumstances? When you find yourself inclined to reject a chance to help, ask yourself why. Examine your reasons for refusing an opportunity to help. Remember that, unlike Simon, you have a choice. When you start to understand why you might be turning away from another's need for help, make an effort to change. Try to remove whatever obstacle keeps you from responding to that need. When you are next faced with an opportunity to help another whom you would have normally rejected, make an effort to reach out and pick up the sliver of the cross that you are being asked to carry.

Questions for Thought and Discussion

FOR PERSONAL REFLECTION

What crosses have you been forced to carry in your own life? What does it mean to you that Jesus is at your side during these times?

FOR GROUP DISCUSSION

What does the world say about carrying crosses and suffering? How do we, as Christians, respond?

SIX

VERONICA WIPES THE FACE OF JESUS

Veronica, The Sixth Witness

Then Jesus said to them, "You will all become deserters because of me this night; for it is written, 'I will strike the shepherd, and the sheep of the flock will be scattered.'" MATTHEW 26:31

S he is silent. She is often silent, but in this wild crowd her silence is unusual. Yet no one seems to notice her. This is something she is accustomed to. She does not stand out in a crowd, or anywhere for that matter, because she does not seek to stand out. For much of her life, she's wanted nothing more than to be left alone. She has no companion, although no one else here seems to be alone. She has never had a companion, and that's the way she has always wanted it. She is a large, strongly built woman, not attractive, and there were no marriage offers after the halfhearted attempt of one young man twenty years ago who wanted the dowry her father would have settled on to have her married and out of his house. She'd flatly refused her parents' pleas, and though they might have forced her, they knew by then the strength of her silent will. Forcing her into marriage with some weak boy would have just brought them all shame; she would have never even tried to make herself into a good wife. She had known from a very young age that she would not be suited to marriage, and because she had been the youngest child of her parents in their old age, she had managed to keep what she thought of as freedom.

No one observing Veronica's life would have thought her free. The people who had long since stopped bothering to speculate about her certainly didn't think her free. To them, the price she'd paid for her strength, her stubbornness in refusing marriage, had been high. She'd ended up caring for her parents as they became older, nursing them even on their deathbeds while her brothers and sisters claimed it was her responsibility because she had not done her duty and gone into another man's home as his wife. She had not complained even as her parents became more demanding and needful. When they had died, her mother two long years after her father, her brothers and sisters had insisted on selling the family home, saying she was not due any greater share of the proceeds than any of them. Her eldest brother had offered her a room in his own house, but she had quietly refused, knowing the offer was not made with his heart and that his smug wife would make her life miserable.

She had taken a room in a widow's house in Bethany, not far from where she'd lived with her parents. At first she'd paid the widow in handiwork, for Veronica was highly skilled with a needle. She hadn't been able to work much during her parents' illnesses, but she was now free to ply her needle day and night. The widow helped her, showing the dresses and linens Veronica had made all around Bethany and even in Jerusalem. Soon Veronica had all the work she could produce, and she was content to sew peacefully in her room. Her neighbors and family continued to disparage her choices but no longer to her directly; and for some of them indeed, disdain and pity had turned to admiration, if not for Veronica herself, at least of her skill.

As she stood patiently in the clamoring crowd, she remembered the day all this had changed.

He had come two years past to Bethany to visit Lazarus and his sisters. By then Veronica had been well established as a seamstress, working occasionally for the sisters Mary and Martha. She had always enjoyed gauging the reactions of the two, so very different. Mary's praise of Veronica's work had always been quiet and generous. Martha's approval, though more grudging, had extended to making sure all of her acquaintances and neighbors knew of Veronica's talent; thus Veronica had been made busy by Martha's many friends. Veronica, though she barely spoke to either sister, felt comfortable with both.

She had been delivering festival robes she'd completed for Mary and Martha two years ago when he had come. Martha had been critically examining her robes as Mary softly exclaimed over the beauty of the work, when the slave announced with great excitement, "The Master is coming!" The sisters had reacted differently, but each showed deep pleasure. Martha in her strong, gruff manner had immediately set about readying their home for this evidently honored guest, while Mary had gone out to meet him. Veronica, curious about the man who could inspire such a response, had slowed her steps in leaving. Expecting some wealthy and powerful Jewish leader—for the family was rich and well-regarded among Jews of both Bethany and Jerusalem—she had been surprised to see Mary and Lazarus greet a lone traveler, dust and dirt from the journey still clinging to him. The greeting had been joyful, as though of a close family member, and yet Veronica had known this family long enough to be familiar with all its branches. This man was unknown; like her, he stood apart. No matter how effusive the welcome offered by Lazarus, Mary, and Martha—each in their own way—this man still knew himself to be utterly alone.

That was what struck her with a force that made her pause in her departure. She felt his aloneness so keenly that her own heart had trembled for him, more than it had ever grieved for her own solitude. She had been rooted to the spot, unable to stop watching, unable to move. At that point, as they drew closer to the house, Jesus looked over at her.

That look of comprehension, of recognition, of compassion beyond anything she had imagined, much less experienced, pierced her very soul. The solitary anguish he bore was so much greater than what she'd known, yet she felt instantly that hers formed the smallest part of his. Observing that something was transpiring between her beloved guest and her favorite seamstress, Mary began to move toward Veronica, intending to introduce her to Jesus. But Veronica understood that everything that could ever have been known between her and this man had already been experienced in that one glance.

She fled.

But today, she would not flee.

Since that day she had been aware of Jesus' growing reputation. She had heard her widow and her friends, and almost everyone she encountered, talking more and more about him. Veronica had long since discovered that people spoke freely in her presence because, to them, it was as if no one was there. She'd heard about his miracles, teachings, and outrageous baiting of the Pharisees and scribes. She'd heard of his kindness and goodness. She'd been among those in the crowd when he brought Lazarus out of that tomb and reunited him with his stunned sisters. In all this time, she never came near to him again; nor did they exchange a single word.

She'd known always that it would all lead to this day.

She had stealthily watched the temple guards go into Gethsemane. She had seen his men desert him in terror for their own lives. She had followed them back to the High Priest's house and again when they went to Pilate. She had watched when they dragged him to Herod's palace and back again. She'd seen him, each time, more beaten and bloody, more stooped and staggering. She'd seen him forced to wear the purple, and she'd seen the thorns crushed onto his head. She'd eaten no food and drunk no water or wine through this vigil. She'd been preparing for it for two years.

And now she could see him stumbling toward her, pressed on all sides by the mob, most jeering, some watching, a few weeping. They meant nothing to her, and she did not exist for them. She took the cloth from the folds in her robe, the cloth she had set aside, the perfect square of linen that she had cut and hemmed and softened. She knew she was a strong woman, and she was prepared to use her strength now.

He drew nigh. She said softly, "Master." Through the din he heard the one soft voice that spoke with love. He raised his eyes, for he could not raise his head. He knew her immediately and tried to smile. She darted forward, startling the nearest soldier and pushing him off-balance. Veronica knelt in front of Jesus and tenderly pressed the cloth upon his bloody, sweat-soaked face.

Veronica and Us

We know even fewer facts about Veronica than we know about Simon. But there is one thing we do know that differentiates Jesus' two "helpers" on the road to Golgotha. While Simon was compelled to help, Veronica chose to help.

And that reveals a world of difference.

While later generations have come to revere Simon for his hard work carrying the cross of Jesus, Simon did not risk his life in following the Roman soldier's command. When you think about it, Simon was simply following an order by the occupying army; he would have been risking his life to refuse. The Romans could not blame him, because he did what they demanded. The Jews who sought Jesus' life could not blame him for helping Jesus, because he had no choice but to follow the Roman command. And the few in that crowd who loved Jesus could have been nothing but grateful to Simon.

But Veronica's was another story altogether. The Romans would have, at the very least, shoved her out of the way as quickly—and probably roughly—as possible.

The Jewish leaders who had betrayed Jesus would have taken note of this bold woman who dared challenge their authority by helping the one they'd condemned. Those who loved Jesus might well have wondered who this woman was and why she was acting apart from them. She was not with the weeping women, she was not with Mary and her few companions, she was not with the beloved disciple, and she was certainly not with the rest of the disciples, cowering in some dim room nearby.

Veronica knew the risk of punishment from virtually every side, and yet she chose to act.

I think we all *need* Veronica. I think we take great solace in knowing that on that darkest of days, when everyone had deserted our Lord, this unknown woman with no historical past and no recorded future was determined to be there for Jesus. She defied everyone and everything, every brutal soldier, every convention, every instinct of self-preservation.

We need Veronica not only to comfort ourselves with the belief that at least someone was willing to reach out to Jesus, but also as a model. Once Mother Teresa was asked how she could take the risk, for herself and her working Sisters, of touching people who were contagious and rejected by the rest of the world, people who were dying horrible deaths, people with leprosy and other physical and mental diseases. She answered that every time she looked at one of these, she saw the face of Jesus. Not only was Veronica the first to touch the ruined face of the condemned and dying Jesus; she was the one who set the bar for the rest of us. And it is very high.

Prayer

Jesus, my Lord, help me to take Veronica as my model. When I go out into a world teeming with people in pain, imprisoned, people who are hungry and homeless and rejected, give me just a fraction of the strength of the woman who risked everything just to gently, momentarily, wipe your face. Lord, give me courage! Help me to realize that it is not enough to tell myself I would have done the same as Veronica had I been in her place; help me to know that I am in her place, here and now, wherever there is suffering. When I take comfort in knowing that Veronica was there for you, help me to understand that I am called to give that same comfort to others. Lord, teach me to be fearless in your service, knowing that, in serving others, I serve you. Amen.

Questions for Thought and Discussion

FOR PERSONAL REFLECTION

Has there been a time in your life when you saw suffering and chose to act—without thinking about the consequences? What do you suppose motivated you?

FOR GROUP DISCUSSION

Have you ever had a strong intuition about someone you didn't know? How did it work out? How can we recognize Christ's hidden work in our lives more clearly?

SEVEN

Jesus Falls the Second Time

A Roman Soldier Accompanying Jesus, The Seventh Witness

After mocking him, they stripped him of the robe and put his own clothes on him. Then they led him away to crucify him.

Matthew 27:31

L
ucius is furious with himself. *What is wrong with me?* he asks himself savagely. *Have I become soft as a woman in just an hour or two?* And because he cannot reveal his frustration, and certainly not his vulnerability, in this mob, he has to restrain himself from kicking the prisoner. Lucius knows that it is this one causing him to feel so disturbed, but he doesn't know how, and he doesn't know why, and he surely doesn't know what to do about it.

So instead he shouts at the thief who bears the cross ahead to move faster. Lucius feels he has been on daylong marches that did not seem to take as long as this stagger to Calvary. The sooner this is over with, the sooner he can resume his life. And it has been a good life, he assures himself, as he marches at a painfully slow pace beside this wretched man from Nazareth. Without speaking a word, this Jesus is making Lucius' stomach clench and his thoughts disarranged.

All his life, Lucius had known he would be a Roman soldier. His father had fought under the greatest Caesar, his sister had been married into another soldiering family. His mother was the daughter of a centurion. This was his fate, his destiny, and until today he had been content, proud of his work.

Yes, certainly, he had been disappointed when he learned that he would be sent to Jerusalem and stationed under Pontius Pilate. No Roman soldier rejoiced at going to the east, and Jerusalem, though a busy city, was a rebellious outpost far from the intrigue and indulgences of Rome. In this desert filled with people who rejected both Roman customs and Roman idols, Lucius would not find the wine and food he was accustomed to as a scion of a respected Roman family. There were no ribald and joyous festivals with days of competitions, gluttony, and debauchery. And, most of all, there was no water. None to speak of, anyway, for Lucius had been raised among the great Roman baths, cisterns flowing with water, water for cleansing, water for farming, water for cooking. Water so plentiful that no one even thought about it. But here, in this austere, forbidding land, water was a precious commodity, and he felt its absence keenly.

But at twenty-five years old, Lucius had accepted the posting as a challenge. He knew that the eastern empire, particularly Judea, was where a soldier's career could be made, or broken. He had traveled south and east eagerly, a year ago, determined to prove himself worthy, anxious to show his loyalty to Caesar by working to quell the rebellions and see that the Roman tribute was efficiently collected. He had forced himself to adapt to the hot, arid days and the nights when the air seemed cold enough for snow. It had never occurred to him that Rome would fail in the desolate east, only that he wanted to be part of the empire's success. He had known of soldiers who had come back from the east to parade through Rome wearing the laurel wreath, but he had known of others who had returned disgruntled and resentful, muttering about barren lands and ungovernable people. Lucius had decided long before he began the journey to Jerusalem which group he would belong to. Even after he had experienced the gut-clenching spectacle of his first crucifixion, that of a Zealot who had led a riot against Rome, Lucius had become hardened against the brutality, reminding himself that the Hebrews were intractable and needed stern lessons if they were to be kept in check.

Today, all his former confidence is gone, and this terrifies him. He glances at the man staggering beside him, barely able to keep moving despite the massive Cyrenean bearing the greatest weight of the cross. Immediately Lucius averts his gaze again. Every time he looks at the Nazorene, he is thrown into confusion. When he considers what this Jesus has endured in the past hours, it is no wonder he can hardly keep on his feet. In a lifetime of soldiering, Lucius had never been so affected by a prisoner's punishment as he had in watching Jesus silently endure the flogging through which Pilate had hoped to win his battered freedom for him. Not once did Jesus cry out for mercy. The most hardened of the Roman cohort took notice of this; Pilate appeared deeply affected by it.

And Pilate's reaction to this one had not been lost on Lucius. His own leader, the procurator appointed by Caesar for his iron-hearted willingness to do whatever was necessary to secure the region for Rome, had blanched at condemning Jesus to death. Lucius had seen Pilate pale under skin browned and weathered by the sun. At the time it had seemed unbelievable to Lucius when he realized that Pilate was actually trying to *free* the Nazorene!

Only now, assigned to march Jesus to the cross, does Lucius understand what Pilate had felt. For this Jesus is all but dead, and yet there is still an indescribable strength, and to Lucius' unbelieving eyes, almost a light exuding from his battered form.

Suddenly, Jesus lurches forward and falls to the ground, curling around himself like a child seeking to escape a nightmare. Lucius hears a groan, and realizes with a sick, cold stab that it has come from his own lips; Jesus remains silent. It is only the Cyrenean behind Jesus who keeps the cross from falling and crushing him.

"Get him up," commands the centurion, staring steadily not at Jesus, but at Lucius.

The coldness spreads through Lucius and yet he feels sweat run freely under his tunic; thus far he has managed to avoid touching the Nazorene. The centurion continues to stare dispassionately at Lucius, as if he knows exactly what the younger soldier feels. Ashamed, Lucius reaches out to haul the prisoner up, but suddenly Jesus moves in a spasm and grasps one of Lucius' hands between his own.

The flash of panicked fury that causes Lucius to start to curse and yank his hand away passes instantly, replaced by a feeling that he has never experienced, much less imagined. As Jesus grips his hand with surprising strength, Lucius is transported. No longer in the narrow, crowded street, he is moving rapidly through moments and places that change almost before he can comprehend them. He sees people at war, soldiers like himself, and though sometimes they do not wear the armor of soldiers, Lucius knows them. He sees men of Africa fighting men with light skin; men from the east fighting men from the west; fur-clad men of the north fighting men of the empire. He sees men and knows not from where they come, but everywhere they battle violently, perpetuating ghastly acts upon each other, women, and children. He sees chariots slicing opponents in two. He sees the elephants of India stomping hapless fighters into the ground. He sees people, families, enslaved and brutalized, and then he sees them freed and returning violence for violence as they savage their own enemies. He sees weapons that he cannot conceive of—what they are or what they will do—until he sees them dropped from metal birds in the sky to burn the people and cities upon which they land. He sees one of these cause an entire city to disappear before the cloud of smoke finishes rising. He sees women fighting beside men just to return to their rubble-strewn streets, their ruined homes, just to claim what is left of theirs. He sees and sees and sees until he is weeping desolately over the sights he is shown against his will.

And then Lucius sees this man, Jesus, in the midst of all of it, also weeping, coming toward him, arms open to comfort him. He realizes that in everything he's seen, Jesus has been present, comforting, healing, holding, bearing away the lost souls, helping those who must remain. In everything he is present, grieving for men and women, offering them himself.

The Roman Soldier and Us

Have you ever wondered, as I have, whether any of the Roman soldiers or the temple guard who were with Jesus in those horrifying hours between when he was taken at Gethsemane and when he was put in the tomb were changed by the experience? It is easy to think that they were, that they *must have been*, because we know that the whole world was changed in those hours. We know that *now*, but did any of them understand that *then*? For many of them, it could well have seemed just another day at work. The Romans were proficient at crucifixion; history tells us that they had perfected the practice. Their enemies lived in dread of a crucifixion sentence in part because it was agonizing and in part because it was meant to confer shame and disdain upon the victim.

So the Roman soldiers, like soldiers right up until our present age, could well have been convinced that they were doing their jobs, doing what they had been sent to Jerusalem to do. And as for the temple guard, the zealous among them probably believed what their high priests and the Pharisees told them: that Jesus had to go because he did not follow the established religious order and because only his death would keep the Jews safe from further oppression by Rome. Add to that the fact that none of the temple guards or Jewish leaders had to actually participate in the actual crucifixion, and it's possible to believe they were relatively unscathed by the events of that day—at least *on* that day.

But I think that there were some among the soldiers and guards who were moved, changed, indeed transformed, by their experience of Jesus in his last hours. How ironic it is to think that in the final hours of his sacrifice the men with him were not disciples, brothers, friends, but the dispassionate men of war who knew so little about him. They were the ones who breathed the same air he breathed, who put their hands upon him, who clothed and unclothed him, who moved him, who sat by him in the waiting hours. I believe that by the end of their time with Jesus, not every touch was a shove, not every word was a curse, not every directive was a snarl, not every mind was shuttered, not every heart was closed.

How are we affected by Jesus in his passion? We cannot imagine ourselves as cold and unresponsive as we imagine the soldiers with him must have been. We cannot imagine ourselves so, or, perhaps, we don't like to imagine this. But as we go about our days, our lives, just trying to do our jobs and mind our own business, as Lucius and his colleagues were doing, are we so very different? Are we open to the profound, and sometimes disturbing, opportunities we are given to learn from Jesus on the Calvary road? Are we too frightened to even acknowledge such opportunities? Do we close our eyes, ears, and minds at the first sign of something that might throw us off our narrow path? Do we close ourselves off from simple compassion because it hurts too much to feel even a little? Is the risk of accompanying Jesus on this devastating journey too high for us to take?

For many of us, the answer may well be yes. That short walk to Calvary is still too long. But that doesn't mean we shouldn't at least take the first few steps—just to see where God leads us.

Action

Today, fall down—in public, in private, getting out of your car, at work, at home, at church, at the grocery store, while doing chores. Obviously the point is not to hurt yourself, so don't hurl yourself onto the ground. And if you are physically unable, don't risk this; you can do this exercise by lying in bed or collapsed in a chair. But if you are able, take a "planned fall." Though Jesus didn't plan to fall three times on the way to Golgotha, he certainly planned to take that journey. It was one of the main reasons God came to earth. When you take your planned fall, make a strong effort to fully experience it. Feel yourself falling and imagine—or remember, if you've actually fallen in the past—the loss of control, that brief stab of despair, the "Oh no!" that races through your consciousness. Feel the weight of your body as it hits the ground. Feel its cumbersomeness; feel the fragility of your bones and how easily your skin might have been cut or bruised by gravel or anything sharp. If you have the courage to fall in any sort of public setting, feel the embarrassment, the sense of people pitying you—or worse, judging you somehow weak or incapable. If you are in a private setting, imagine how you'd feel if people were watching. Once on the ground, take the time to perceive the world from your diminished condition. What does it feel like to be down upon the earth instead of walking or driving or moving over it? What does the world look like from your position? How does it feel to be looking up at people or your environment instead of encountering everything at eye level? Stay where you are for a few moments to fully experience your position. Consider what it will take to rise up again, how your body will need to work and coordinate each of its members. Now, imagine how much harder that would be if you were weak, beaten, carrying the sins of the world on your shoulders, and rising up only to go to your death.

Questions for Thought and Discussion

FOR PERSONAL REFLECTION

Can you name a time when you were "sent," perhaps against your will, to a difficult place or situation? Looking back, how was Jesus present for you?

FOR GROUP DISCUSSION

The Roman solder is given a wider, more universal view of wars and violence that goes beyond his experience, and yet still he sees individual suffering. How are Christians called to respond to the violence, terror, and war in our own age?

EIGHT

One of the Sorrowing Women, The Eighth Witness

A great number of people followed him, and among them were women who were beating their breasts and wailing for him.

LUKE 23:27

They were sisters, of a sort. Not related by blood or birth or even raised in the same home, they were nonetheless of the same family. They were widows and unmarried women and the indulged wives of powerful men. They took as their ancestresses Miriam, sister of Moses, who helped lead the Hebrews out of bondage in Egypt; Deborah, who judged Israel; Esther, who saved her people from almost certain extermination in the Persian Empire; Judith, who saved her people by seducing and then destroying the most powerful pagan warrior known to the world. They were women of Judaism, whispering prophets, women of faith, women who came together in Jerusalem to worship in the temple, to await Yahweh's deliverance, to seek the Messiah.

And now that they had found him, his own people were about to kill him.

Leah knew that some of her sisters had lost faith. They had argued that if he were Yahweh's Christ, he would not be allowing this to happen. Yahweh's Christ would not appear only to allow himself to be crucified by the oppressor Romans. Yahweh's Christ would have convinced the Jewish leaders of his identity, not allowed them to collaborate with Rome on his condemnation. Yahweh's Christ would have destroyed the oppressors and cleansed Jerusalem of parasitic leaders and priests.

Thus did some of Leah's sisters argue, and they are not here today. They have remained in their own homes, grieving and lamenting and wondering how long they will have to wait. Those who are here with her today still believe. They may have no clear answer for their disappointed and bereaved sisters, yet their own faith persists. They believe without understanding.

Leah's faith in Jesus of Nazareth is founded in something more, something she has never related to these sisters, something she has never revealed to anyone. She had known Jesus was the chosen one from the first time word of him reached Jerusalem. For years, she had cared for her ancient aunt, the prophetess Anna; it was from her that Leah had inherited her devotion to Yahweh, her longing for the Messiah.

It was from Anna that Leah had learned that the
Messiah had been born and was walking the earth. The
older Anna became and the less frequent her forays into
the temple, the more she spoke to Leah of the child. She
spoke almost with a desperation, determined that Leah
should know that the Messiah lived among them, some-
where. It was as though Anna feared that if she did not
teach Leah well enough, all would be lost. A prophetess in
her own right, Anna had always hoped that she would live
to see the infant she'd blessed in the temple shortly after
his birth come into his own, as Yahweh's Messiah must.
She had clung to life for much longer than it would have
seemed possible, all in the hope of seeing Jesus once more
in all his glory.

Again and again Anna told Leah of the day, now over
thirty years past, when she saw the young family in the
temple. "I was drawn to them without knowing why," she
would tell Leah. "Anyone could see that they were poor—
by their dress and the humility they showed in the temple.
They had come to offer tribute according to the law for
their firstborn son. When I came to them and saw the
child, I knew. Not by appearances or human sign or word.
But I knew from God. That this was the beloved, this was
the Messiah."

"They named him Jesus," Anna would say urgently,
gazing intently at Leah to make sure she understood. "His
mother's husband was named Joseph, and they planned to
make a home in Nazareth. Watch and listen for one coming out of Nazareth called Jesus."

Anna had died ten years before Leah heard word of a
rabbi from the north who was shocking the Jewish hier-

archy and delighting the people. "But what is his name?" Leah asked one of her sisters, one whose husband did business in Galilee and had actually seen the man.

"He is called Jesus," her sister had answered, "of Nazareth."

Now, as they wait on this devastating day for him to pass, Leah remembers the past three years as if only three days had gone by. Whenever Jesus came to the region, she and her sisters would go to hear him. He was not what they expected in a messiah, and yet so much more than they could have imagined. He did not preach a kingdom of war through which the Romans and all enemies would be purged, but a kingdom of God where oppressors would have no power, and violence no place. He confounded the scribes, Pharisees, and Saduccees and gave hope to the carpenters and fishermen. He chastised the priests and moneylenders and ate with criminals and prostitutes. He debated with the learned, but then chose twelve unknown and barely educated men for his closest companions.

He traveled and talked with women. He even defended them.

It was this that made Leah hold her tongue when she and her sisters discussed Jesus. She never told them what she knew and *how* she knew, because she'd realized as soon as she first encountered Jesus that she no longer believed because of Anna, but because with her own mind and heart and soul she knew Jesus was the one.

Now the crowd around her stirs, growing louder and more restive. There is a narrow turn near where she stands with the sisters who remain faithful. They are all weeping, but Leah dries her eyes now and stands tall. She wants him to see her faith, to know that she knows. But when Jesus stumbles around the corner, pitching to one side until the African steadies him, she recoils despite her intentions. He is so broken! She had seen and heard him speak just a few days ago; he'd been so vital, so intent, so strong. Today she can hardly recognize her Lord. She hears the sisters behind her wail and keen at the sight, but she gathers her strength and keeps her eyes steady upon him.

He sees them too, and with an immense effort he straightens his body to look upon them. He looks into Leah's eyes and smiles wearily at what he sees. Yes, recognition, but he is beyond this now. He pauses, and Leah is surprised that the guards allow this, but the young Roman closest to him looks away, as if refusing to notice, as if ashamed. Jesus gazes upon their grief and tears, their ravaged faces and swollen eyes.

The Sorrowing Woman and Us

And he says, "Daughters of Jerusalem, do not weep for me, but weep for yourselves and for your children. For the days are surely coming when they will say, 'Blessed are the barren, and the wombs that never bore, and the breasts that never nursed.' Then they will begin to say to the mountains, 'Fall on us'; and to the hills, 'Cover us'" (Luke 23:28–30).

We hear a lot in our world about End Times, that period of time that some believe is described in the Book of Revelation and that is to immediately precede Jesus' return to judge humankind at the end of the world as we know it. Just about every time there is a storm, earthquake, war, or any kind of serious human-made or natural disaster, we hear theories suggesting that the End Times are upon us or, at the least, right around the corner. Many people seem fascinated by this concept, to the extent that we have best-selling books, movies, and plays about it. One could argue that for a culture founded on respect for life, we are somewhat obsessed with how and when it will end.

This is nothing new. Jesus himself talked about what we've come to call End Times, usually when badgered by disciples and followers to tell them when it would happen. But despite his assurances that there would be wars and storms and any number of events leading up to this period, he decisively explains that only God knows when the end of human life as we know it will be.

By all accounts, the time leading to Jesus' return will not be pleasant. Why, then, do some feel so anxious for it to come, or so determined to judge that we are living through some stage of this period? Is it that we believe we are ready to be judged? Is it that we are convinced that we will shine while others may suffer?

Jesus, rising for a moment out of his own physical and spiritual anguish, cautions the faithful women of Jerusalem against thinking that what they are witnessing in his Passion is the end. They may *want* it to be the end; they may feel so grieved and mournful and even righteous in their own faith that they feel they are ready for life to end, but Jesus makes it clear that the time has not yet come.

No one can be certain that it has come upon us, either. For all of the pain and sorrow and violent events in our world, can we really say that there is more brutality now than at the time when our Lord was crucified? Or, for that matter, at any time between then and now? If the end was not 2,000 years ago or 1,000 years ago or 75 years ago, why do we think it might be now?

Perhaps, like the sorrowing women, we are not called to spend our lives predicting or anticipating the "end." Jesus' journey to Calvary suggests that women in particular are called to be strong enough to stay with him as only the women disciples did on that desolate day. We are called, like them, to do our best to live in faith *today*, with the hope for tomorrow. And in so doing, we can pray that God will continue to delay final judgment until we all more fully live our lives in acknowledgment of Jesus' sacrifice.

PRAYER

*Merciful God, give me the discernment to perceive the Way of the Cross not as an apocalyptical symbol or a reason to despair, but as a revelation of your love for humankind, and for me. Help me to take every step with those disciples who had the courage to be there, knowing that every step will lead me closer to you. Teach me to rejoice not in your suffering, but in the compassion that made you willing to suffer for us. Give me the humility to accept that I need all the time and grace you see fit to give me to make myself more ready for you. Show me ways through which I can live my life not in a frenzy about the End Times but in faith about **this time**. O Lord, give me a measure of peace in and through you! Amen.*

Questions for Thought and Discussion

FOR PERSONAL REFLECTION

What do you, like Leah, long for? What are you watching for in the future?

FOR GROUP DISCUSSION

Name someone in your life who has been a guide or prophet for you, as Anna had been for Leah. What has this person taught you about Jesus?

NINE

JESUS FALLS THE THIRD TIME

The Widow Who Put her Last Two Coins in the Temple Treasury, The Ninth Witness

He looked up and saw rich people putting their gifts into the treasury; he also saw a poor widow put in two small copper coins.

LUKE 21:1–2

She is in a hurry. She has asked her mother-in-law to keep an eye on her young son, and she doesn't want to impose on the older woman any more than necessary. After all, her husband's parents had taken her in when he had died last year, even though they had barely enough for themselves. And she knew that every time her mother-in-law looked at her little boy, she saw the face of her own dead son when he had been so young.

She had seen the same expression of both love and pain on her mother-in-law's face that she felt on her own when she watched her little one.

Today of all days, when her mother-in-law had the added work of preparing for the holy Passover Sabbath, was not the best time to leave the older woman with the extra task of chasing the toddler around their small home, but it was her only option. She felt compelled to reach the temple, to place her offering in the treasury box, to share the Passover blessing God had provided. Just a few days ago, she had come to the treasury with the last of the money her husband had earned for them before falling sick and dying. After paying the physicians, there had not been much left at his death, but she'd made it last as long as she could, contributing to her mother-in-law's expenses whenever she would permit it. Earlier this week she'd taken the last of it, blessed Yahweh for having provided for them, and contributed those remaining few coins to the temple box. She had told her mother-in-law what she planned to do, and the older woman had agreed. Yahweh would provide, she'd said.

And he had. No sooner had she returned home that day, trying not to think about how they would survive, then her mother-in-law had returned from the market, greatly excited. The landowner in whose fields her husband had worked was asking after her! He had unexpected guests coming for Passover and needed someone to help his wife prepare the house and the meal. Would she be willing?

Would she?! The two women danced around the small room that served as their home as the little boy looked on in wonderment at this uncharacteristic display of merriment. After a moment, he'd tried to join them, twirling around in a circle until he fell unceremoniously on his little rump. At which both women had laughed until, of course, they'd cried.

As her mother-in-law had hoped, the landowner and his wife had been so pleased with her work that they'd hired her to work in the house and kitchen for a few days every week, and though she suspected it was more out of kindness and sorrow for the loss of her husband than out of need, she'd grasped on to the offer as the gift from God that she knew it to be. Now she was hurrying to the temple to make a thanksgiving offering from the money they had paid for her work this week. She knew she could have waited until after this festival Sabbath but something in her told her to go this morning.

Yet now she finds herself hemmed in by the crowds, and although she knew there would be many worshipers today, these people are not penitents or those who have come to give thanks. They are restless, excited; a few are grieving; more are angry. She tries to make her way through this narrow, bending street in order to reach the temple, but she is forced along in the flow of bodies. Frustrated, she spies a small opening and darts through, but her foot catches on a stone and she pitches forward. As she tries to scramble to her feet, anxious about the crowd, she looks up and sees him fall.

He does not fall as she has fallen, trying to regain her balance even as she goes down. There is no panicked, embarrassed look in his eyes because he fears making a spectacle of himself before others. He does not put his hands out in front of himself to try to break the impact of the fall or protect his head and face.

No. He simply falls. Hard.

And there he remains, flat on the ground, the weight of the cross upon him for a long moment before the African behind him struggles mightily to pull it off him. Seeing the cross, she suddenly understands the crowds, what it is she has stumbled into, and she is even more anxious to get away. She rises to her knees, ready to flee. But the man does not move. She can see that his eyes are closed. At first she thinks that he has hit his head too hard and has died on the way to his own execution. It passes swiftly through her mind that this would be more merciful for him. This is not your affair, she tells herself, and again begins to rise.

Then Jesus opens his eyes and looks at her. She sinks back down beside him, recognizing him instantly.

This is the rabbi who had shocked her three days ago by calling attention to her gift at the temple treasury. At first she had been ashamed, thinking he would ridicule her for the paltry sum she was offering, but his words had stunned her. He told his disciples and all who would listen, "Truly I tell you, this poor widow has put in more than all of them, for all of them have contributed out of their abundance, but she out of her poverty has put in all she had to live on" (Luke 21:3–4).

Her face had flushed and she'd been overwhelmed with many emotions in that moment. "How can he know this about me?" was her first thought. Her second had been then, as it was now, to flee. She was not accustomed to being noticed, much less praised—if indeed, the rabbi named Jesus was praising her, for at that moment she had not been sure, and so she hurried away from that place.

But now as Jesus lies unmoving except for his eyes

searching hers, she cannot bring herself to leave. Behind the mirror of pain in those eyes, she sees a resignation and still something else: the same gentleness that had been in his gaze the last time before she'd run away. Flooded with compassion, she whispers urgently: "Stay! Refuse the suffering that awaits. You are hurt and exhausted beyond bearing. Release your spirit now to God. Suffer no more!" A light flares in his eyes and then dims, replaced again by that wordless, sorrowing certainty. She reaches to touch his face, but the centurion bellows an order and she feels herself snatched away from behind and shoved against the close wall. Crumpled there, she watches in anguish as Jesus draws a shuddering breath and begins with excruci-ating slowness to take command of his body. She sees him struggling to make his limbs work when they no longer hu-manly can. She seems to feel his every nerve, tremor, and spasm as she watches helplessly. She witnesses him rise, trembling, first to his knees and then, roughly helped by a silent young Roman soldier, to his feet. The cross is again laid upon him, but she can see that the African does his best to bear the greatest weight.

When Jesus is upright, he pauses, summoning strength that is no longer there. He looks upon her one more time, briefly, but her own eyes are blurred with tears. And then he moves forward.

The Widow and Us

The story of the poor widow startled me as a child, perhaps because in my parents' Bible, it is accompanied by an illus-tration of a very young woman carrying a plump (in other words, heavy-looking!) toddler in one arm and dropping her last coins into the box with her other hand. She is thin, as though the child has been fed at his mother's expense, and solemn, as though fully aware of what she is doing. She seems to be carrying the world on her shoulders. The story and illustration stood out for me for a number of reasons.

First, in the illustration she is young, and when I was young, I didn't expect widows to be young. It struck me to think of her, not as a pious old woman sacrificing her last few pennies toward the end of her life, but as a young woman still in serious financial need for all the expenses she had, and would have.

Second, she is serious about what she is doing. She knows what it means to give away this money; she knows how much she needs it; she knows she is making a sacrifice. She is not making some dreamy, ecstatic gift; she is, as Jesus points out, dropping all that she has in a box for the temple, dedicated to God. This is no whim; it is a faith-filled decision.

Third, she shows no interest in Jesus and the disciples. The illustration depicts Jesus and the disciples off in a corner while she is in the foreground making her gift. Jesus is gesturing toward her as though to illustrate the point he is making, but she is intent on what she is doing. In other words, she is not looking for attention or praise. In this way, she is very much like the perfect giver Jesus describes when cautioning the disciples against giving alms publicly so that everyone can see. The poor widow has no interest in being noticed. She is living day-to-day, and she is living for and through God

Fourth, although she sounds like a character in one of Jesus' parables, with her, Jesus is not telling a parable; he is seeing and describing a truth. For the most part, Jesus taught in parables, but every once in a while, he saw something that offered the opportunity for a "living lesson." He observed just this sort of model in the poor widow. He knew her as soon as he saw her, and he knew exactly what she was doing.

In this way, too, he knows all of us, what's in our hearts, and exactly what we are doing. And that's where the story of the poor widow gets a bit discomfiting for us. Jesus selected this living lesson deliberately, and one of the reasons may well have been to shock us out of our complacency. Of all the learned and wealthy and generous people in the temple during that Holy Week, whom does he draw attention to? The one person who is doing something that almost none of us will do: giving all we have to God.

Such a thing not only requires smiting us where we can be hurt the most—our wallets—but also smiting us where we can also be hurt pretty badly: our pride. The widow is giving all she has because she believes that God will provide for her. This is not a suicide gesture; she does not then go off in a corner and wait to die. She goes off to live with utter trust in God, knowing that God is everything to our nothing, that God provides everything to our need. So Jesus gives us the model of a woman both parting with precious money and expressing herself to be wholly in God's hands. She is willing to do what we often find so hard: she acknowledges her utter vulnerability, her complete dependence on God.

But surely, we reassure ourselves, God doesn't mean us to give everything away?!

I tell myself the same thing, but in certain quiet moments, when I go most closely to the bone of what Jesus asks of us, I wonder. And then I am grateful for God's patience and, even more, his forgiveness, as I try to move a little closer to the person I can only be through his grace.

Action

Take out your wallet. Count the paper and coin money in it right now. In the next twenty-four hours, try to give that money away. If you feel you can't give the entire amount away, stretch yourself as far as possible to give away as much as you can, and maybe a little more. Keep in mind that this amount is probably not a fraction of your assets, and imagine how you would feel if it was all you had. Envision how it would feel to love and trust God so much that you could give it all away. Imagine yourself wholly dependent on God. However you contribute the money— whether to your church, a nonprofit, an organization fighting an illness, beggars on the street, or a friend or acquaintance—focus on dedicating the gift as a symbol of your love for and dependence on God.

Questions for Thought and Discussion

FOR PERSONAL REFLECTION

Has there been a time in your life when you had to accept kindness, help, or even outright charity from others? How did it make you feel?

Have there been times when you felt your gift to God was paltry, small, or weak? What does Jesus say to you at these times?

FOR GROUP DISCUSSION

How do our weaknesses link us to something larger and stronger than ourselves? What practical ways can you see this at work in the church today?

TEN

Jesus Is Stripped of His Garments

A Soldier Casting Lots, The Tenth Witness

When the soldiers had crucified Jesus, they took his clothes and divided them into four parts, one for each soldier. They also took his tunic. Now the tunic was seamless, woven in one piece from the top. So they said to one another, "Let us not tear it, but cast lots for it to see who will get it." This was to fulfill what the scripture says, "They divided my clothes among themselves, and for my clothing they cast lots." And that is what the soldiers did.

John 19:23–25

M arcellus really wants that tunic. One can never predict how the lots will fall, but he has a good feeling about this. The tunic looks warm, and it is the only piece of the man's clothing that is not very bloodstained. But he'd want it regardless, because after four years in this miserable empire outpost, he is still unaccustomed to the climate. Sweltering desert days and then, when the sun sets, it is like a fire is blown out and the sharp, clear cold encroaches. Some nights on patrol, he can see his breath; he still feels amazed when through the cold fog of his sighs he can see palm trees! Palm trees growing in a place where a man could freeze at night!

For him, everything about this place is wrong and foreign, starting with its distance from Rome. Rome was civilization; Judea is an impossible chaos where no one could be truly ruled. In Rome, Marcellus would be respected, a leader of men, a strong husband to his wife and a father to his children. Not that they seem to need him. The longer he is constrained to stay in this untenable land, the harder it becomes to maintain his place in his family. It is his wife's brother to whom his children turn for guidance and attention. Whether his wife had also replaced him is something he cannot bear to think about. He will soon be an old man, and what does he have to show for it?

Every day, Marcellus yearns for home where it means something for a soldier to walk through the streets, a victor from whatever campaign had just finished. Here, he triumphs over nothing. These people cannot be truly conquered. You could beat them and war against them and try to destroy their culture, but you could never break their spirit. Though obedient to Rome, he was not a cruel man and had grown weary of what he'd been forced to do to control these obdurate people. The Jews believed they had existed long before the Romans, and they made no effort to disguise their contempt for the Roman occupiers, not to mention the Roman religion. These people had their One God, and many of them would rather die than bow to any other.

Look at this one! This Jesus, who had endured beatings and humiliation unlike any Marcellus had seen in his years of trying to gain through brutality what these Jews would not give through respect or even fear, is a perfect example of these people. How many times had that puppet, Pilate, given Jesus a chance to save himself, to simply say a word or two in his own defense, and yet he'd done nothing to satisfy Rome or even Pilate's pathetic ego. All Jesus had to do was show a little respect, a little willingness to work with the procurator, but no. He had chosen instead to march to crucifixion, already half-dead, with a thorn vine rammed onto his head.

Marcellus felt nothing for Jesus. How could he even understand something like this? He had looked on dispassionately as the young soldier, Lucius, who seemed suddenly confused, had stripped the man's clothing. Jesus had flinched when the clothes on his back tore at the wounds from the whip, but had not cried out. The tunic was the only good piece, carefully woven with no seam, and when Marcellus had seen Jesus' mother reach out to him on the way, he sensed that she'd made it for him. She looked like the kind of woman who would have cared for her son, wanted him to be warm in the cold nights even as he traveled from town to town, spreading dissension and revolution. If Marcellus felt for anyone, it was for this mother, and for all the mothers of these men who could not seem to keep themselves from challenging Rome, from bringing violence upon themselves and their families. Did they ever think about the suffering, the retribution, they were calling down upon their mothers and fathers and sisters and wives and children? Marcellus had seen the suffering of Jesus' mother, and in that moment, he'd felt compassion.

It was gone now. As he joined the other soldiers, gathering to cast lots, the centurion gestured toward Jesus and said to him, "Marcellus, you've been with this one from the very start. Almost like one of his followers!" Confused, Marcellus looked up at his superior whose laugh was a short bark. "You've forgotten? Three years ago, not long after you arrived, we were both assigned to watch the wild man, John, who was washing people in the Jordan. Remember? The one dressed in hides and eating only what the land had to give him? Herod feared John, and so he came to the attention of Rome. He made a lot of noise until Herod finally silenced him. But we were there the day he met this one."

Marcellus remembered. He had been in the eastern empire for just about a year and was already feeling the disillusionment that had only grown since then. They were just a small cohort sent to try to intimidate the Baptizer and those who would come to hear his ravings and be bathed by him. Though he'd shown no sign at the time, Marcellus had been surprised at how impressed he was with John's words. Though considered dangerous by the Jewish and Roman authorities, John had not spoken of insurrection, instead exhorting the masses on how to live properly. Marcellus had been particularly interested in what the wild preacher had told the soldiers in the crowd: "Do not extort money from anyone by threats or false accusation, and be satisfied with your wages" (Luke 3:14).

Marcellus had been in the region long enough by then to know that discipline had broken down among the soldiers, and many thought it completely within their rights to bribe and steal from the people they ruled. For the most part the centurions looked the other way, thus encouraging the general dissipation of the Roman guard. It was as though the wildness of this uncultivated land had infected the Romans, broken down their sense of law and organization. The irony of a fiery Jewish preacher instructing the soldiers to do what they should have been doing under Rome anyway was not lost on Marcellus. And when, in the ensuing years, his growing bitterness had driven him to consider bribery, he'd resisted, unable to forget John's words.

The last day they'd been sent to watch John at the Jordan, something unusual happened. A stranger had approached John, and when Marcellus saw the fearless preacher step back, he moved closer, interested in why John was so abruptly quiet. John had talked to the stranger, apparently refusing to baptize him, another thing that perplexed Marcellus. Eventually the stranger prevailed, and John lowered him into the water. Marcellus was observing the stranger closely when the light came, and the voice.

"You are my Son, the Beloved; with you I am well-pleased" (Luke 3:22).

Marcellus had tried to forget the man, the voice from the heavens, the Baptizer, all of it. He convinced himself that it was thunder, or some trick from John's followers. Only now does he realize how well he had forced the scene from that day out of his mind. He stares at Jesus, stripped and wounded, and recognizes what he doesn't want to see. Marcellus looks back at the tunic and is paralyzed by the memory of the first day he saw it. He drops his lot and puts his head in his hands.

The Gambling Soldier and Us

In looking for signs, betting on signs from God, we can lose sight of that fact that God is right in front of us

"It must be a sign," my aunt said when we missed our plane because of traffic. "God did not want you to get on that plane."

The only sign I saw that day was that of my father, gripping the steering wheel as we sat in airport traffic as though by tightening his grip on the wheel, he could tighten his grip on the words he was just itching to say to my aunt. Fortunately for the sake of family peace, he managed to hold them back.

Some of us tend to be big on signs from God. This plane incident was not by any means the only time I heard in my family and among my friends about waiting for—or betting on—a sign from God. If such and such happens, it means we should make that decision. If this thing occurs, that means God is not happy with us or something we've done. If we see this or that, it means that God *is* happy with us or something we've done. If we see no sign…well, that in and of itself is a sign that God is not speaking to us at the moment.

In our search for signs, we are, much like the soldier, gambling with God. Is this really such a great idea? If we cannot discern what God wants from us through reading Jesus' teachings in the gospels, prayer, or meditative listening to God, then we are surely not going to discover God's will because the path of a plane seems to fly across the sun, or because the seventh car we pass is the same color as the first car we bought decades ago, or because our favorite song comes on the radio as we are driving to do something we are not sure we should do. When our grocery bag breaks on the way up the stairs or in the parking lot, it doesn't mean God is upset with us. When we make all the lights and get to church on time, it doesn't mean God approves of a particular decision. In fact, we don't need a sign to know that we are in no position to gamble with God.

What we gamble with when we rely on such things is not God but superstition.

Does this mean that God does not speak to us through and in our lives? Of course not. God is with us always, around us always, in the world always. God is everything, always! But to the extent that we gamble on signs, instead of simply depending on God's presence and Holy Spirit consistently in our lives, we are really depending upon our own interpretations of God. In other words, we pretend to rely on a sign from God while in reality we are moving the agenda in one direction or another.

This puts us at risk of following in the footsteps of Marcellus. We are so focused on gambling over a thing, of imbuing a thing with the power of God, that we fail to see God right in front of us, all around us, in complete control. We miss the reality of Jesus, the comfort of the Holy Spirit, the majesty of God.

Prayer

Almighty God, Father, Son, Spirit, forgive me for the times when I am so afraid, so desperate, so confused that I look for specific signs of your approval or presence. Forgive me when I gamble on things rather than rely on your constant love and mercy. Forgive me when I assign power or meaning to events that have none simply to affirm my own agenda. O Lord, it is hard to acknowledge that I am completely powerless before you, that I am nothing and that you are everything! It is harder still to celebrate that truth with trust and patience and even silence! Help me with this, Lord! Help me not to search for signs when I am fearful or confused or panicked. Give me discernment, and more important, give me peace. Teach me that during the dark nights of my soul, you are there with me, and that I need no sign to prove your presence. Amen.

Questions for Thought and Discussion

FOR PERSONAL REFLECTION

Where do you need approval in your life?

Do you ever assign meanings to signs, rather than trust in God's plan for you?

FOR GROUP DISCUSSION

In your experience, is there a need among the Christians you know (including you) to seek God's approval? What practical things can we do that can help us surrender to God's love and mercy?

ELEVEN

JESUS IS NAILED TO THE CROSS

A Slave with a Hammer, The Eleventh Witness

Pilate also had an inscription written and put on the cross. It read, "Jesus of Nazareth, the King of the Jews." Many of the Jews read this inscription, because the place where Jesus was crucified was near the city; and it was written in Hebrew, in Latin, and in Greek. Then the chief priests of the Jews said to Pilate, "Do not write, 'The King of the Jews,' but, 'This man said, I am the King of the Jews.'" Pilate answered, "What I have written, I have written."

JOHN 19:19–22

I t takes a great deal of strength to nail a man to a cross. The spikes must be driven with great force, not in the palm, but somewhat below in the wrist where the bones are strong enough to bear the weight of the body for several hours. To do it right requires skill and precision and power.

The slave has such strength. He prides himself not

only on his strength, but on his ability to drive the spike through skin and bone and into the wood with one blow. To use more than one blow forces the victim to suffer additional anguish upon already excruciating pain. And though the slave has long since hardened himself against the suffering and shrieks of the victims, he has no wish to make it worse. To do so would be inefficient, beneath him. He considers himself an expert, a professional.

While he has a great understanding of pain and the human body, rivaling that even of a physician, he has no compassion. Though he has lived for almost three decades upon the earth, he cannot ever remember feeling compassion or sorrow for another human being, much less for himself. If he had as much understanding of the mind and spirit as he has of the body, he would understand that most of what could have been human in him was beaten out of him before he was even old enough to recognize it. But he has no such understanding, and if it were offered to him now, he would refuse it. What good would it do him? How could it help him?

He cannot remember a time when he was not a slave. He cannot remember a mother or father, except for a vague idea that he was told once or twice that his father had traded him to slavers for a few coins. He cannot remember the names of many of his masters over the years, just the very few who treated him better than the animals they kept. As masters go, the Romans aren't the worst. They bought him when he was already strong, already dead to all feeling; and because he has served them well, they feed him his portion and treat him decently. He is seldom beaten, most likely because even the brutal and well-armed soldiers don't like to think of what he might do should he waken from his closed and narrow mind and start to feel anger. Or anything.

He is massive. They think of him as the sleeping giant, the tamed monster, although he does not know this. He is to them like a wild, savage creature, but he is their creature. They sometimes gamble on what feat he will be able to accomplish when they set him to it, and this he does know because those who bet and win often are generous in rewarding him. They enter him in competitions, fights to the death, and he has killed many. As with those he has nailed onto crosses, he does not think about these men, though he tries to kill them quickly. He knows that he could earn enough to buy his freedom, but he has no wish for freedom. He does not know what it is, and the life he has is the one he lives.

But here is something new. This man is the first the slave has fastened to a cross without screaming and struggling violently against the tight bindings that hold the arms against the wood until the spikes are driven through. When the man does no more than let a guttural gasp of agony escape at the first blow, the slave pauses to look at him. But his eyes have rolled away in pain, and the slave sees nothing in them. So he waits for the man to begin to strain against the bindings, to fight for life, but the man does not. The slave cannot understand this, but he feels an appreciation of the man's courage. For the first time since becoming a slave of the Romans, he wonders why this one must die. The man's eyes return and look upon the slave, and what the slave sees there causes something unfamiliar and disturbing to stir in him. The slave moves swiftly and surely to the other arm; he will be quick and careful with this one, determined to cause no more pain than must be.

When he finishes and is about to raise the cross up, the world-weary soldier Marcellus strides over and hands the slave a thin board with writing. "Nail this above him first," orders the soldier with an urgency in his voice that the slave has not heard before. Without knowing why, the slave asks Marcellus, "What does it say?" Making no effort to hide his surprise at the question or the man asking it, Marcellus meets the slave's gaze and says, "Jesus of Nazareth, the King of the Jews."

The slave stares mutely at the sign he now holds in his hand. Marcellus observes him keenly and then slowly begins to turn away. "I have never been to Nazareth," says the slave as if to himself, and the comment is so utterly uncharacteristic that Marcellus turns back to him. "It is a blasted village to the north." Marcellus waits.

"Is he a king?" The slave nods toward Jesus, noticing that Marcellus will not look upon the man.

The slave hears Marcellus breathe in sharply, but before the soldier can answer, the centurion barks, "Nail the sign on and pull up the cross. What is there to talk about!"

Marcellus steps back, reluctantly, and the slave, kneeling over the man again, is loathe to strike the smaller spike in the wood about his head. The blow upon the wood of the cross will jar the man and there will be a new wave of agony, a precursor to what he will feel when the slave lifts the cross. The slave can see that the man is watching him, and, not knowing what his own face is doing, he offers the man a small smile.

"I think you are a king, then," he says quietly.

Then the slave lowers his hammer, turning it so that the flat surface rests upon the nail he holds against the wood above Jesus' head. Trembling with the use of all his strength and weight, the slave pushes the nail gently with the flat of the hammer, penetrating the wood without even a tremor upon the cross.

And the king smiles back.

Later, after he has lifted the cross and seen the spasms of pain pass across his king's face, when, in the normal course of his life's events, the slave would have taken his pay and left the place, he instead settles nearby to watch. His masters, except for Marcellus and the agitated young one, Lucius, pay no attention to him. Nor does he expect them to. His eyes are on his king. Though the women standing nearby weep, most people pass by and jeer at him, but his king is in the midst of his own suffering and takes no notice. This reaction the slave understands. One of the thieves, the one who struggled and shrieked curses most violently against the slave's work driving in the spikes, also mocks his king; yet of this, too, Jesus takes no notice. The other thief, however, is angry, and the slave hears him speak. "Do you not fear God, since you are under the same sentence of condemnation? And we indeed have been condemned justly, for we are getting what we deserve for our deeds, but this man has done nothing wrong" (Luke 23:40–41).

The slave approves of these words. He sees the good thief turn to his king.

"Jesus, remember me when you come into your kingdom" (Luke 23:42).

And for the first time, the slave hears his king speak:

"Truly I tell you, today you will be with me in paradise" (Luke 23:43).

"I have never been to paradise," the slave says, as though to himself, but he thinks, looking up at his king, that he would like to go there.

The Slave and Us

It's hard for me to think about how often I hurt Jesus. Any Christian who's spent a Good Friday afternoon or evening in church, or walked the Stations of the Cross, especially those of us who do this year after year, has a keen sense of how Jesus suffered. We've read accounts, seen depictions, watched plays and movies, listened to music. The very thought of what Jesus went through—the sheer brutality, cruelty, betrayal, abandonment, physical agony—can make us cringe in horror. There are reminders all around us, throughout the year. Every time we walk into a Catholic church, we see a crucifix, some of which are detailed in ways that are painful to even look upon. We give our children crosses to wear around their throats or in their ears to mark sacred or otherwise important events like First Communion, confirmation, graduation. We've been told again and again that Jesus' suffering was not just for the people of his time, or for those who came before, but for all of us. Jesus suffered so that all of us could be forgiven, transformed. We know that we must be people of the cross before we can be people of the resurrection.

So how do we face up to the fact that, despite what Jesus did for us, we continue to sin, continue to contribute to his suffering, his crucifixion?

Despite all we've been taught, all we believe, all we've

instinctively come to feel about Jesus' suffering for us, we
sometimes act in ways that add to it rather than acknowledge it. In this we are like the slave. Willing victims of our
human nature, our fears and our anger, we shut our mind to
Jesus' sacrifice for us so that we can open ourselves to sin.
We do not ever (hopefully) set out to hurt Jesus, but when
we hurt others, when we hurt ourselves by turning from
God, we do indeed pound our own nails into the cross.

How then, can we live with ourselves as Christians? We
can't. Which is why we don't rely on living with ourselves;
we rely on Jesus' compassion, on God's forgiveness, on
the Holy Spirit's encouragement. We rely on grace. We
acknowledge that, like those who crucified Jesus, we are in
constant need of forgiveness. Unlike those who crucified
Jesus, we know we need this forgiveness, and we know that
we must live in a continual state of repentance, ready to
accept God's forgiveness and grace, both being our spiritual sustenance.

Like those few who were with Jesus on the road to
Calvary who were truly transformed, we need to experience Jesus' suffering to fully understand the scope of his
forgiveness, the gift of his grace. And we need to experience it not only as witnesses and co-sufferers with Jesus,
but as witnesses and companions to those who suffer in
our age. The cross is perhaps the most startling and stark
symbol of not just compassion and forgiveness but empa-
thy. If Jesus could suffer and die for humans and because
of human nature, we must, at the least, share the suffering
of those in our lives and our world. Because when even a
sliver of the cross becomes our own, we more fully comprehend both its weight and the cost of adding to it.

Action

If you don't have any nails in your toolbox or junk drawer, go and buy some. At the start of the day, place a small box or bag of nails in your briefcase, bag, pocketbook, or in a dish or jar on the kitchen counter. Be aware during the day of your thoughts and actions regarding others. Every time you think or act compassionately, remove a nail from its container and leave it in a neutral place like your desk, a shelf, or a dresser. Every time you think or act in an unfeeling or hurtful way, remove a nail from its container and put it in your pocket. At the end of the day, gather the nails from both your compassionate pile and your pocket, and study them for a moment or two. Remember some of the acts and thoughts that built each pile. Keeping them separate, place them by or under a cross or crucifix in your home. Ask God for forgiveness for the one; thank God for the grace that built the other. In the morning, pick them up, mix them up, and start again.

Questions for Thought and Discussion

FOR PERSONAL REFLECTION

▧ *Have you ever experienced a time when someone seemed numb to your suffering? How did you respond?*

FOR GROUP DISCUSSION

▧ *Think of one or two habits you do every day that are automatic, that you don't think much about. How might Jesus transform these simple actions to bring you closer to him?*

TWELVE

Jesus Christ Dies on the Cross

A Soldier Who Pierces Jesus' Side, The Twelfth Witness

Then Jesus gave a loud cry and breathed his last. And the curtain of the temple was torn in two, from top to bottom. Now when the centurion, who stood facing him, saw that in this way he breathed his last, he said, "Truly this man was God's Son!" **Mark 15:37–39**

A tilius has been observing for hours now with a practiced eye. In the end, as always, it will all come down to him. Not Pilate, not the soldier who did the flogging, not the arrogant centurion who thinks himself superior, not the pathetic little worms who had betrayed these victims; no, not even Caesar! Nor would the brutality of the cross finish the job. In the end, he knows that at least the two men will die at his hands. He, Atilius, is the one who will end their trembling lives. It is he who will be looking into their eyes when the light dies. The one between them, he may not last.

For all his years in the eastern empire, it had been this way. It often took these recalcitrant Jews and Samaritans, these rebels and criminals, so long to die. And Rome didn't have forever to wait. One of the most efficient governments in the known world could not wait around for stubborn Jews to finally give in to the inevitable. Rome had perfected crucifixion, providing a very public and very humiliating lesson, not to mention a prolonged and painful death. It was a death meant to teach all those who might consider opposing the empire. And while Rome had succeeded in striking terror into the hearts of any potential rebel or criminal who witnessed a crucifixion, the empire had not succeeded in making it an efficient death.

Indeed, muses Atilius, one eye always on his victims, the two were incompatible. A swift and clean death—say, by lance, arrow, or even flogging—would not offer the public spectacle that crucifixion provided. Thus, it would not demonstrate to prospective rebels and lawbreakers Rome's willingness to punish in the cruelest fashion devisable.

Still, in the end, after enough suffering had been witnessed, after even the most brutal among the soldiers were sated with watching the contortions of their victims, after the most vivid of lessons had been taught, Rome would be done with waiting.

And that's where Atilius came in. He was highly skilled in the breaking of bones. He considered himself quite the equal of sculptors and painters who focused on the human form. Could they possibly know more about the human body than he? Its strengths and weaknesses? He doubted it.

Atilius well understood both the facts and the process of crucifixion. A crucified man who had enough leverage to put weight upon his ankles or feet could live for a surprising length of time. If he had been strong before he'd been condemned, and if he'd not lost a great deal of blood from the inevitable floggings and beatings that preceded crucifixion, it could take hours, even a whole day to die. Atilius remembered one man who had lasted an entire day and night and into the next day. He had been a powerfully built, rugged man who'd been sentenced to death for joining a rebellion of the Zealots, yet another misguided band of malcontents who were deluded into thinking they could best Rome. Not only had that Zealot hung on the cross longer than any of Atilius' other charges, his legs had been the most difficult to break.

For this is how Atilius brings death: by breaking the legs of the crucified man. Atilius removes that last obstacle to death, the ability of the victim to put enough weight on his feet to keep breathing. Once the legs are broken, the victim smothers. A large, muscular man himself, Atilius prides himself on being able to end the suffering of the victims with his own two hands. He believes that by using his hands, he offers a more honorable way—both for himself and the crucified—to bring death. He considers use of the large, unwieldy mallet a method of last resort. But if need be, and he *had* needed it with the massive Zealot, he knows precisely where and how to deliver the blow.

The circumstances under which Atilius might be summoned to facilitate death vary. The cohort might be needed elsewhere and can no longer be spared to guard Golgotha. Or, those being crucified may not be important enough to draw a crowd, thus losing the opportunity to teach a long, indelible public lesson. Or the centurion might grow tired of the wailing, keening women who come to watch their condemned men die. Any number of reasons might call for death to be dealt more swiftly.

Today, Atilius had been told well in advance of this moment that he would be needed. The Jewish chief priests, some of whom had been complicit in the condemnation of the one in the center, want the bodies removed before sunset for yet another of their sacred festivals. Atilius himself cannot be bothered with such details. Why did the Jewish leaders condemn one of their own when their enemies Herod and Pilate were already killing Jews daily? Atilius does not care. Who, after all, can begin to comprehend these people, this land, the untenable labyrinth that is Rome's eastern empire? All he knows is that the bodies have to be removed before sunset, and for the bodies to be removed, he must do his work first.

Atilius is vaguely aware that some of his fellow soldiers are growing restive. Young Lucius and hardened Marcellus, who should be triumphant after winning the Nazorene's fine tunic, seem particularly distressed; even their centurion has been casting an anxious eye upon the darkening sky. Storms do not bother Atilius. They sweep down upon this land regularly and are gone just as swiftly. Why should this threatening sky portend anything different? He can break bones as easily in the rain as in the sun.

Suddenly, the one in the center cries with a loud voice, "Eli, Eli, lema sabachthani?" (Matthew 27:46).

"What does it mean?" Atilius asks Lucius curiously, for there is desolation beyond fear or pain in the Nazorene's voice that penetrates Atilius' focus. But the younger soldier simply fixes his eyes upon the cross in a mixture of terror and comprehension. Atilius grasps his arm, repeating the question. Lucius, without taking his eyes off Jesus, whispers, "My God, my God, why have you forsaken me?"

All strength drains from Atilius, and his mind fails him. He is conscious of a sensation unlike any he's ever known. It is as though an abyss has opened in the very center of his being, his body hollowed out until there is nothing left but a gaping blackness into which he feels he must fall—*is* falling. There is no lowering storm sky above him, no rocky earth below his feet. He can find nothing to fix upon; his life as he has known it is meaningless. At the last, when he feels that he is lost, his eyes are drawn to the one who has cried out. Atilius' eyes lock onto Jesus as his arms might lock onto a sturdy log in the midst of a storming sea. Jesus is not looking at Atilius, but the soldier will not look away from the face of the Nazorene. And there, Atilius sees the desperation pass away, replaced by a peace—and yes, a joy—that Atilius cannot comprehend but will spend the rest of his life trying to.

Finally, as Atilius does indeed watch the light die out of Jesus' eyes, he understands that he will never break the bones of this one, for in the end, God has not forsaken him.

The Soldier with the Lance and Us

How often does life deaden us to the reality of Jesus Christ?

Daily we look right at him, in the breathtaking beauty of the world he has created, in the searing poverty of so many of his creations, in everything in between. But like Atilius we don't see, or we refuse to see. Atilius, at least, has the excuse of not knowing Jesus; we have no such excuse. But in other ways, it is harder for us to acknowledge the reality of Jesus… *because* we know him and we know what he asks of us.

Jesus Christ is no longer a revelation for most of us. He is a reality, and a reality that demands much of us in the midst of a world that is already demanding, it sometimes seems, too much. He demands not only that we take time from our busy-ness to attend to him and his word, but even more: that we bring him and his word *into* our busyness, that we incorporate him into our daily lives, that we, in fact, build our lives upon him, the cornerstone. He demands that we live in and for him.

And when work and family and all the big and little crises of our lives are clamoring for attention, this can seem impossible. It's one thing for Jesus to ask us to set aside a few minutes for prayer, an hour for Mass, a meditation now and then, even an annual retreat. But to live in constant awareness of Jesus' presence and teachings? Who can do this?

Why do we find it so difficult to live in and for Jesus? I think it is because, ultimately, what Jesus asks of us is love. To love him, yes, but also to love others, which is where we, self-protecting little creatures that we are, naturally balk. Jesus' many adjurations, admonishments, and commands that we love one another are the most difficult stumbling blocks in our efforts to live in and for him. It's easy to love God in the abstract, but to love one another? Daily? Hourly? Moment to moment?

Why do we find it so challenging to see the face of Jesus in those around us, much less the most deprived and depraved among us? Perhaps it is because the face of Jesus that we cannot help but see is not the face of the smiling Jesus at the Cana wedding, or the teaching Jesus sitting with the Samaritan woman, or the healing Jesus with Jarius' daughter, or the gentle Jesus blessing the children, but the suffering Jesus, his face bloody, bruised, and contorted in physical and emotional anguish, crying out from the cross: "My God, my God, why have you forsaken me?"

Perhaps that is the face we confront in the poor and desperate and sick, and it is a face we fear to look into or come close to, never mind to touch or stroke in comfort. Perhaps that is the face, that even when we close our eyes tightly, stick our fingers in our ears, and hum a loud, toneless tune, we cannot escape. Perhaps that is the face we fear to see in the mirror.

But consider this: what a comfort it is to know that Jesus cried out these words on the cross! If Jesus, God's true-born Son could feel this way, then it's OK for us to feel this way! We don't have to hide our fear that God may abandon us. We don't have to pretend we are not afraid, alone, desperate at times. We don't have to deaden our senses to those emotions in ourselves or in others. Because God himself, in the form of a Son in the throes of death, felt them and shouted them out.

And he was heard then. Just as we are now. And always.

Prayer

Jesus, embodiment of God's word, sacrifice of God's love for all creation, Messiah for all humankind, help me to live in and for you. Help me to know that you are with me even when everything in life conspires to make me feel that you are not. Help me to remember that when God seems most distant, it is because in my own fearful blindness, I fail to see how close God is to me. Help me to understand that it is only my own weakness and fear that makes me think God is inaccessible, hidden from me. Help me to never turn away from my own pain and anguish, or that of others. Help me not to run when I recognize your suffering face in another, or in myself. Help me to remember that love was not crucified on the cross, but was indeed born there as surely as in a Bethlehem cave over thirty years earlier. Amen.

Questions for Thought and Discussion

FOR PERSONAL REFLECTION

▨ *Have you ever felt that God had forsaken you?*

▨ *Looking at the world around you, who are those who might feel forsaken by God, and by others? What can you do for them?*

FOR GROUP DISCUSSION

▨ *How are you called, as a community, to walk with those who feel abandoned or forgotten?*

THIRTEEN

JESUS IS REMOVED FROM THE CROSS

A Young Woman with Mary, The Thirteenth Witness

There were also women looking on from a distance; among
them were Mary Magdalene, and Mary the mother of James the
younger and of Joses, and Salome. These used to follow him and
provided for him when he was in Galilee; and there were many
other women who had come up with him to Jerusalem.

MARK 15:40–41

I do not watch them take my Lord down from the cross. It is not because I can't bear to watch, for what could I see that would be worse than what I have seen, without once looking away, these past hours? Every moment of agony is indelibly impressed in my mind's eye; to see him now is nothing more than a relief that the suffering is over.

110

No, I do not refuse to watch them take him down, but my eyes are now needed elsewhere. I have borne his suffering with him the best I can, and now I must try to bear his mother's with her. Thus, my eyes turn to Mary, for she is the reason I live now. Otherwise, with my Lord gone, we are all merely waiting to join him in death.

It is through his mother that I came to know him. When Mary was preparing to leave Nazareth to travel with him, she came to my parents' home. I was helping my mother bake bread, and as usual, there was nothing but silence between us. There had been little else between my parents and me for as long as I could remember. They were not bad or cold-hearted people; they were simply worn out by the burden of trying to feed and marry off four daughters in a village struck by poverty and oppressed by Roman and Herodian taxes. I think that every time my mother looked at me, she revisited the hopes she'd had as a girl and experienced again their death by the reality of life with my father in Nazareth. I think she saw that my sisters and I would become as she was, and that was something she did not care to look upon.

And what did my father see when he looked at me? A second-oldest child, who had been born a girl despite his prayers for a boy—an indication that perhaps he would not have sons though he would try for them twice more—another mouth to be fed, another girl to be married off despite no money or goods to offer the family of any potential husband. In me, my father saw the first of many disappointments.

At that time, when my Lord was starting to attract interest in Nazareth and Galilee, when Mary had decided to be with her son as often as possible, my parents were negotiating with an older man who was willing to marry my sister. Willing, but not eager, and certainly not in love with her. My father was trying to think of something he could sell to buy my sister this unpromising marriage. How she felt about it did not matter; my parents were pathetically grateful to any man who would take the first of their burdens away.

So when Mary came to our house that morning, I was the last thing on my father's mind. She greeted my mother and father and then said simply, "I am going to be with my son. I would like to take your daughter to help me." I held my breath in the corner: which daughter? And then she looked directly at me, nodded, and gave that small, wise smile of hers. I wanted to go with her more than I had ever wanted—or ever will want—anything in my life. I would like to say that it was because I wanted to follow her good and wonderful son, to serve and learn from him. But in those days, such good intentions were not mine. I would like to say that I loved and respected Mary, and so wanted to be her help and companion along the journey. But those were not my first thoughts. All of those thoughts and intentions came later. At that moment, all I wanted was to leave my parents' home, to leave desperate Nazareth, to leave behind the life I had and the future I expected. All I could think about was the grim, aged face of the thirty-five-year-old farmer who was halfheartedly asking for my fifteen-year-old sister in marriage.

I was thirteen years old.

My father looked at Mary blankly. My mother barely lifted her head from the grey lump of dough she was kneading. My heart fell. They were going to refuse. I could see it. How could they find me a husband if I was traveling the country, following a man who was already stirring excitement and animosity among all who heard him? What good girl would choose such a path; what proper parents would allow it? In Nazareth, Jesus had aroused little more than suspicion, and my parents, though exhausted with their own worries and inattentive to my Lord and his mother, were not unaware of the general reaction. I could see by the way my mother ignored Mary, by the way my father turned half away from her, that the answer would be no.

And then Mary spoke again. "I have money."

My mother's hands stopped working. My father turned back to the slight woman standing just inside our doorway, and an ugly, desperate light leapt into his eyes. I looked away. But though I was hurt by what I saw then in my parents, I was not surprised. In just a few words, Mary had provided them with an answer to two of their biggest problems: where to find the means to marry off their first daughter and how to at least temporarily rid themselves of their second. Suddenly Jesus' and Mary's reputations didn't matter quite so much to my parents. Nor did mine.

"How much money?" My father made no effort to hide his need, his greed.

Mary brought out a small cloth bag from inside her robes. "Fair wages for a year," she said, raising the bag toward my father. "And the same for every year she is with me."

For years, almost since Mary had returned with the child and her husband many years ago, there had been rumors in Nazareth that the carpenter's family had money put aside. The family never lived in a way that signaled wealth. Indeed, Joseph had been one of the humblest men anyone could remember in our village, and Mary was always kind, always quiet. But there had always been something about the family that made others keep a little apart from them. The notion that they had money was just a part of this, and Jesus' growing reputation had only added to the mystery. No one knew these days how the rumors started or whether there was any truth to them. But they had persisted over the years, and Mary's offer of the bag of gold seemed to confirm them.

My father had not hesitated on that day, almost three years ago, after the gold appeared. No one had asked me what I wanted or how it felt to be sold by my parents, but I think Mary could see from my face that I was both hurt and excited. She was tender with me from the first day I joined her, never referring to me as a servant, which is what I was and am, but always as her companion.

Why did she pick me? Of all the girls in Nazareth, why me? I have asked her many times, but she only smiles and replies, "Why not you? Who else?"

Now she calls me daughter.

In these final days, I have missed her smile. I have watched her face grow old over these years, but in this last week, it has lost all semblance of joy. Even five days ago, when my Lord entered Jerusalem in triumph, Messiah to all but the elders and chief priests, Mary was somber. She watched the adoring crowds anxiously, and for the first time, I saw the smallest trace of bitterness as she listened to the screams of praise.

I understand now that she must have known, as did my Lord, that it was all leading to this—that some of those very people who were shrieking words of adulation would within days be crying for blood. And now their latter cry has prevailed.

I watch her face as she opens her arms to take his body. Though no more than ten years older than my mother, Mary's is an elderly face now, marked by the harsh sun and wind, furrowed by laughter and more recently fear, now ravaged by weeping and agony. The rain has stopped, but her face is wet. It is a face sculpted by love that is almost unimaginable, and savaged by the pain such love brings.

I help her bear the weight of his body, so thin and yet now so heavy. Her hands tremble as she touches his cheek, stroking it as she must have done when he was a child. With exquisite care, she untangles the thorns from his hair as though she could even now keep them from hurting him. She does not notice when she cuts her fingers, once, twice, again.

My eyes are on her face; hers are on his. After a time she reaches out and gently, gently closes my Lord's eyes. And then I see that small, wise smile through her tears, and mine.

Mary's Companion and Us

I think it may be impossible for us to fully comprehend the death of Jesus and what it meant to those who loved and followed him. After all, we don't have to think too much about it, do we? We know the "rest of the story," and it doesn't bode well for death in general and certainly not for Jesus' death. Scripture, movies, historical records, and the Stations of the Cross give us at least a vague concept of how Jesus suffered, but it is easy for us, except for an hour or so on Good Friday, to avoid thinking about Jesus' actual death. We know it was a "temporary" death, and we don't have to spend a great deal of time contemplating its impact on the people of his time.

It was devastating.

As much as Jesus suffered in the hours before his death, we can't begin to comprehend how those remaining suffered in the hours afterward. Imagine giving up everything—your money, your family, your job and career, your home—all to place your hope in a man. A man who, by the way, was not a scholar, had no evident means of support, did not work, was not a priest or elder, held no government position, and had virtually no power as power is defined by the world.

Not only have you given up everything tangible, you've given up your heart and soul. You are crazily, madly, insanely in love with the man. You cannot imagine living without him, without his presence, without his words, without his companionship.

Then, the powers of the world—which you have abandoned and rejected—surge forward and take him from you in the bloodiest, most decisive, seemingly irreversible way possible. And next, they're coming for you. What do you do? Whom do you turn to? Where do you hide? How do you live according to what he taught you? How do you hold onto your love, your faith, in him?

How do you mourn for him?

I think for us to truly experience Jesus, we have to spend time sitting with Mary and his family, friends, and followers in those dark hours between 3 PM on Good Friday and dawn on Easter Sunday. Obviously, we prefer not to; it's much easier, much lovelier, to be amazed and delighted at his teachings and miracles, or overwhelmed with joy at his resurrection. But to fully live the gospels and the resurrection, we need to spend time focusing on his apparent absence.

When we allow ourselves to feel the desolation of his loss, we can better value the blessing of his constant presence in our lives. We can become more compassionate people, both with ourselves as we confront spiritual "dry patches" or experience the loss of loved ones, and with others as they face loss and grief. When we allow ourselves to suffer with Mary and those who loved and seemingly lost Jesus, we are better able to appreciate the "losers" in this world—and that is what many who suffer grief or trouble today are called.

Like Jesus, we are not called first to joy before we are called to suffer as we acknowledge and confront our own losses and the losses and despair of others.

Action

Choose to mourn with someone. Is there a person in your life who has lost someone precious or important to him or her? It could be someone close to you like a good friend, family member, or neighbor. It could be someone you don't know as well as you might (or could, or should) like a work colleague, fellow parishioner, hair stylist, barista, committee acquaintance. It could be someone like your mail deliverer, child's teacher, classmate. The list of people in your life, when you really think about it, is a lot longer than at first consideration. If anyone you know is experiencing a loss, find a respectful, caring way to grieve with and for that person. What you do specifically will depend upon how well you know—and are known to—the individual. The companionship you offer someone close to you will be different from the respectful kindness you offer the person you do not know well. Part of the challenge of this exercise is to give careful consideration to what this person may need from you. Don't try to tell this person you know how she or he feels, because even if you think you do, you don't. Instead, find a way simply to demonstrate your sorrow for their sorrow, your sadness for their pain, your care for their grief. Understand that when you mourn for and with another, you have yet another opportunity to recognize Jesus, both in temporary death and in eternal life.

Questions for Thought and Discussion

FOR PERSONAL REFLECTION

▧ *Whom in your life have you disappointed? Was it the result of something you had no power to change, or was it within your power and desire, yet you chose not to act? How can you move forward in love and compassion?*

FOR GROUP DISCUSSION

▧ *Who is disappointed within your community, and why? What steps can you take toward reconciliation with them?*

FOURTEENTH

JESUS IS LAID IN THE TOMB

A Slave of Nicodemus, The Fourteenth Witness

Nicodemus, who had at first come to Jesus by night,
also came, bringing a mixture of myrrh and aloes,
weighing about a hundred pounds. They took the body of Jesus
and wrapped it with the spices in linen cloths, according
to the burial custom of the Jews. JOHN 19:39–40

I know why my master insisted on trying to carry the heavy burden himself. Guilt. He feels guilty because he was able to do nothing to save the young rabbi. My master blames himself for the fear that kept him from trying to stop the Sanhedrin, Annas and Caiphas, and the others from betraying Jesus to the Romans. My master made some effort to save him, but in the end, he could not bring himself to stand firm against the plot. When the chief priests turned on him and accused him of believing in Jesus like the rest of the rabble, my master lost heart. And his nerve.

Because he did, indeed, believe in Jesus, and if the elders who accused my master knew how often he sat with the young rabbi, hidden in the darkest part of the night, who can say what they would have done to him? Ejected him from their presence, surely, and if he had survived such humiliation and rejection, what else might they have done? Look at what they did to Jesus!

Of course Nicodemus was afraid. Who can blame him? Certainly not me, and though I accompanied him on those shrouded nights when he secretly found his way to wherever Jesus was, and though I heard with amazement and growing joy the words of the young rabbi, even I would not have found the courage to stand up for him against the Jewish rulers. Jesus spoke about things that have seldom if ever been heard of before in Israel, and yet seemed to be secretly hidden inside me. He stirred my soul up to God.

So I am ashamed to say that I quietly approved my master's cowardice, knowing that if he lost everything, so would I. I was no more willing to forfeit the good life I have with him than he was willing to lose his position and wealth. Thus I did not urge him to go to the secret council, held by the high priest before dawn today. Instead, I helped Nicodemus bar the doors against messengers. I listened to him pace through the bleak hours before dawn and did not go to him with words of encouragement, words I know he wanted to hear from me. I allowed the words of life I heard from Jesus those many nights while I sat silently in the dark at my master's feet to be swept away by thoughts of the soft bed and easy work and good food I enjoy because of Nicodemus' wealth and status. I too am a coward.

And I too share my master's guilt.

But I am a slave and thus a more practical man than my learned master. I knew he could not carry the weight of aloes and myrrh he was determined to bring to Golgotha now that Jesus is dead. Nor could I, not if we wanted to reach the place before they put Jesus in Joseph of Arimathea's tomb. My master and I are both old men, I have been with him for some thirty years, and the days of either of us carrying one hundred pounds of anything are long past. I had a hard time convincing him to pack the spices onto one of his animals; he was that determined to bear the weight on his own. It was only after he made several attempts that I was able to draw him away and direct the other slaves to load the sturdy donkey.

Along the way, my master was silent, miserable. "At least Joseph had the courage to go to Pilate for the body, to prepare a tomb. I had not even that much strength or that much foresight," he muttered, more to himself than to me.

I'd made a halfhearted attempt to comfort him. "Joseph of Arimathea was not at the foot of the cross any more than you were, Master. You have done nothing wrong."

He looked at me with such anger that I feared I had gone too far this time. But then the rage on his face crumpled into a lined mask of despair. "Old friend," he'd whispered hoarsely, "I have done everything wrong."

Now he stands ahead of me, side by side with the Arimathean, as they prepare Jesus as best they can, wrapping his body in the myrrh, aloe, and spice-soaked cloth— two of the most powerful men in Judea, humbled and horrified, ashamed and repentant, gladly doing the burial work that would be normally left to women or slaves. They finish, and Nicodemus motions to me as Joseph calls his head slave. It takes a moment for me to steady myself for touching the young rabbi—he who had been so full of life, now, here, prepared for a stranger's grave. I am relieved to see the wounds hidden, the ruin of his face and body covered in the clean cloths. The four of us shift his body to the bier; and slowly, carefully, we four old men lift the bier and make slow, solemn progress to Joseph's tomb. Sunset is coming, but we do not, cannot, move swiftly.

For the first time in all my days with Nicodemus, we do not joyfully anticipate tomorrow's dawning of this festival Sabbath. Instead, as we enter the dark tomb, I shiver, suddenly afraid that it will never be day again.

Nicodemus' Slave and Us

They were many types of slaves in Jesus' day. The word *slave*, as we read it in the New Testament, could refer to an immigrant worker, an indentured slave/prisoner who might have been either captured and enslaved or who might have sold or attached himself to a wealthy patron, a skilled artisan attached to the estate of a wealthy family, or even a servant who had become like one of the family. In other words, all kinds of people from all walks of life could be slaves, and many of them would have identified themselves more accurately by the terms servants or employees in modern parlance. They served a master, a household, a purpose, a leader, maybe all four at once. For many who took the name, there was no shame associated in being called a slave.

We have a hard time reading anything good into the word *servant*, much less the word *slave*. Our aversion to these words is not only due to our abhorrence of the insti-

tution of slavery, but—much less nobly—to our reluctance
to think of ourselves as subordinate to anyone. We are
proud, independent people who fought for our freedom
and live in a nation that has never been conquered or oppressed. We don't consider ourselves under duress or command or oppression from any person or any nation.

Yet, like Nicodemus and his slave, we are servants of
God, slaves of Jesus, his Christ, and joyful prisoners of the
Holy Spirit. We are indebted and indentured, and if we do
our job right—living according to Jesus' word—we are also
slaves of each other. Sounds preposterous, doesn't it? For
most of us, every fiber of our being strains against the concept of being enslaved to another, never mind *every* other!
It just goes against our grain.

But that's what Jesus did: He went against the grain of
human constructs. He goes against our grain even now.
He stood, and still stands, in the direct flow of human
nature with a simple message: No, you are going in the
wrong direction. Turn around. Don't worry about yourself
so much. Don't waste time and energy hating and fighting
your enemy. Don't worry about your stuff so much. Don't
obsess over food and clothes and jewelry. Don't serve
money. Don't think about what others think of you. Don't
seek honors or chase titles and positions. Don't be a slave
to your fears and anger, your greed and desire, your basest
instincts for survival.

Instead, Jesus calls us to be slaves to him in his life,
death, and resurrection. He calls us to die a little each day
to the world, to ourselves, to our appetites, to sin, so that
we can live a little more fully in his risen life. How shall we
answer?

Prayer

Beloved Lord Jesus, your period of agony came to an end, and you were laid to rest for a while in the tomb. Although I know of the joy that will come with your resurrection—the stunning happy ending to a story that seemed to end so sadly—I ask you to help me spend this time quietly resting with you. Give me the courage to join you in the tomb— unafraid, for I know that joy will come—but contemplating your slavery for humankind. Lord, help me to be quiet with you, to use these hours—the darkest before the dawn—to consider what it means to be your slave, the servant of all. Strengthen my weakness, Lord; eradicate any pride that keeps me from embracing the role you have offered me. Loosen the grip that the world and all its power, wealth, and appetites has upon me. Free me to be with you, my beloved Lord and my beloved God, and to wait with you; and then raise me up too to be your slave on earth, your servant throughout eternity. Amen.

Questions for Thought and Discussion

FOR PERSONAL REFLECTION

▨ *When and how has God called you lately to find rest in him? How has he called you to take action as well?*

FOR GROUP DISCUSSION

▨ *How is your community called to be servant of God right now? How will you respond?*